Issues in Ethics and Applied Ethics Series

Volume-V (Part – I)

Metaethics

Issues in Ethics and Applied Ethics Series

Vol. 1	Ethics in Business, Applied and Environment
Vol. 2	Ethics in Feminism
Vol. 3	Socio-political Ethics
Vol. 4	Biomedical Ethics (Part I)
	Biomedical Ethics (Part II)
Vol. 5	Metaethics (Part I)
	Normative Ethics and Virtue Ethics (Part II)

Forthcoming Volumes

Vol. 6	Ethics of Business and Economics
Vol. 7	Ethics of Charvaka/Lokayata, Morality and Secularism (Part I)
Vol. 8	Ethics of the Jainism (Part I)
Vol. 9	Ethics of the Buddhism (Part I)
Vol. 10	Ethics of Values and Education

About the Editors

Sri Shiva Nath Prasad completed his M.A. in Philosophy from Patna University. After retirement from Government of Bihar, wherein he served in different capacities, started the publication of a bilingual journal of Philosophy, "Abhrant", as editor. Later, on, the persistent request of scholars of philosophy, he started two unilingual journals entitled 'Darshan Digdarshan' in Hindi and the journal of Bihar Philosophical Research, in English. He has authored a book entitled 'Carvaka/ Lokayata an Analytical and Hermeneutic Study' which was published from Janki Prakashan, Patna. Besides, he has edited an anthology entitled 'Phenomenology Methodological Introduction' with VT Sebestian, Panjab University, Chandigarh.

Debashis Guha, University Professor of Philosophy, Allahabad University, is teaching ethics from the very beginning of his teaching career, in Ranchi University. Dr. Guha was awarded Visiting Professor of UGC (1994-96) in Jadavapur University, Kolkata. He was awarded Major Research Project (1997-2001) on 'Applied Ethics in Indian Context', which was published in six volumes, under the series "Practical and Professional Ethics". In addition to it, he also authored a book entitled 'An Enquiry into the Case of Pain and Suffering'. Dr. Guha is internationally known for his books and articles published in national and international journals.

Avinash Kumar Srivastava, Professor and Head P.G. Dept. of Philosophy, Magadh University Centre, Nalanda College, Biharsharif, competed M.A. from Patna University and Ph. D. from Magadh University, Bodh-Gaya, on the topic of 'comparative study of the concept of Samadhi (Yoga) in Early Buddhism and *Bhagavad-Gita*'. He received the research scholarship of Nava Nalanda Mahavihara for his said research. He was awarded Minor Research Project of U.G.C. on the topic of 'Adaptable Nature of Buddhism'. He has authored two books, 'Bharatiya Darshan ki Mool Samasyaen and Living Buddhism'. Besides he has edited three anthologies, 'Ethics at the core of Globalization', 'Bauddha Darshan : Adhunik Sandarbh' and 'Tulnatmak Dharma Darshan'. Dr. Srivastava is a prolific writer and widely known scholar, with more than forty research papers published in India and abroad. He was Joint Secretary and Secretary of Akhil Bharatiya Darshan Parishad, General Secretary of Bihar Darshan Parishad and Vice President of Indian Society for Buddhist Studies. Besides he is member of editorial board of several Research Journals.

Issues in Ethics and Applied Ethics Series

Volume-V
(Part–I)

Metaethics

Edited by
Shiva Nath Prasad
Debashis Guha
Avinash Kumar Srivastava

CONCEPT PUBLISHING COMPANY PVT. LTD.
NEW DELHI-110059

ISBN-13: 978-81-8069-976-4 (Series)
ISBN-13: 978-93-5125-152-1 (Volume-V) (Set)
ISBN-13: 978-93-5125-153-8 (Volume-V, Part-I)

First Published 2018

Published and Printed by

Since 1974

Concept Publishing Company Pvt. Ltd.
A/15-16, Commercial Block, Mohan Garden
New Delhi-110059 (India)
T : 25351460, 25351794
E: publishing@conceptpub.com, W: www.conceptpub.com

Cataloging in Publication Data—*Courtesy:* D.K. Agencies (P) Ltd. <docinfo@dkagencies.com>

Metaethics / edited by Shiva Nath Prasad, Debashis Guha, Avinash Kumar Srivastava.
pages cm. -- (Issues in ethics and applied ethics series ; volume-V, part-I)
Contributed articles.
Includes bibliographical references and index.
ISBN 9788180699764 (series)
ISBN 9789351251521 (volume-V) (set)
ISBN 9789351251538 (volume V, part-I)

1. Metaethics. I. Prasad, Shiva Nath, editor. II. Guha, Debashis, 1956- editor. III. Śrīvāstava, Avināśa, 1955- editor. IV. Series: Issues in ethics and applied ethics series ; volume-V, part-I.

BJ1012.M48 2015 DDC 170.42 23

Foreword

I have read with pleasure different contributions of new and old teachers of moral philosophies in different Universities in this edited work on Issues in Metaethics, Normative Ethics and Virtue Ethics and some applied concerns of ethics. Editors Sarvashri Shiva Nath Prasad, Debashis Guha and Avinash Kumar Srivastava must have been working hard on this project for couple of years. I felicitate them on its completion.

Studies of ethics down from the ancient age of Socrates, Plato and Aristotle, to our modern age refer to normative, critical and metaethical issues. History of Moral Philosophy had its well-known milestones in Western thought by seminal thinkers like David Hume, J. Bentham, J.S. Mill and Immanuel Kant. Lately in last century, we had significant revival of ethical studies in the light of newer departures about analysis of concepts. Cambridge professors Henry Sidgwick and George Edward Moore made novel critique of concepts of Good and the nature of Human Value Concerns. They sought to reconcile contemplative deliberation with moral intuition as well as fusing public utility and rational individualism. This agenda of theirs led to contemporary ethical theories in several original formats.

Besides, these beginnings in our times nature of Logic of moral discourse and Language, kinds of Value Categories and their conceptual articulation and grounds, nature of good-reasons in moral arguments or persuasion marked the various topics making analytical Metaethics, today. These undercut traditional Normative Ethics that was divided on contrast of the Concept Right/Wrong (Deontology, Duty Ethics) with concepts such as The Good

Summum Bonum and various other Goods (Values) that Normative Ethics seeks to formalize in Man's Moral Life in the community of his peers (Teleology). Lately, some philosophical Metaethicists wish to sidestep the above theoretical dichotomy of concepts, i.e., of the Right and the Good. They underline the ethics as deliberation on what they visualize to be the constituents of truly virtuous character or different Virtues that could either together or singly make us the virtuous person. This makes Virtue Ethics particularly sensitive to praxis in specific situations (Acts), rather than the old concerns with general universal Moral Rules/Principles. In this sense Virtue concept emphatically tries to liberate ethical deliberation of these A-Historical Norms or General Principles of conduct that fail to guide in concrete Praxis of living. Actually, the agent faces Moral dilemmas, casuistry, naturally, dominates such Praxis.

For instance, the innate sense of Justice conflicts with our compassion. Indian Tradition furnished several Challenging Moral Dilemmas. Only three, here, are mentioned below, one Yudhishthira in *Mahabharata* faces a moral dilemma about his vow of speaking the Truth while committed to wage his just war against unassailable enemy Drona. Two, Personal Agony of Harishchandra exacting Cremation Fee from his spouse Tara, who is having no money for cremating their own son – child Rohitashva. Lastly, the most controversial dilemma of Desertion by Prince Siddhartha his young and nursing wife Yashodhara and son Rahul at midnight to seek the Middle way to eliminate the generic *Duhkha* of our Human-Condition. Very obviously, despite of passage of aeons from times of Epics, now, today's Existentialism such as of Albert Camus "Outsider" or to Twentieth Century Classic of GE Moore's *Principlia Ethica* the Dilemmas and contrarieties of human Praxis hardly get any better solution. Should one fight for the freedom of one's country over nursing one's terminally sick Mother? Moore argues that intrinsic verities likes of justice, generosity, intelligence, compassion or truth-speaking could never be optimally co-realized. So, we have to make choice of Verities-profile and order and bear the responsibility for the heart-breaks each involves.

Now consider the last letter a character Inspector Javert writes to Prefecture of Paris (*Les Miserabillis,* Victor Hugo's Classical Novel) before committing suicide for failing in his duty to send a Jail Fugitive Jean Valjeon back to prison because he cannot ignore the marvellous great noble deeds the said fugitive has been putting up for the underdogs and wretched of the Metropolis, while he himself, failing in his own duty. He seeks way out of this impasse by committing suicide... Quitted his Existence.

Clarity and conceptual architectonic as different contributors have reviewed with considerable skill in different sections of the present work on Ethics Normative, Analytical, Virtue Ethics of various scholarly schools like Existentialism and Linguistic Philosophy as well as some themes in Indian Moral Philosophies, is monumental. It is comprehensive survey of world's ethics-scholarship. Fabulous, Kierkegaard, Sartre, C.L. Stevenson, Utilitarians Rule/Act theorists Philippa Foot, R.M. Hare, Wittgenstein, GES Anscome are all exposed sufficiently in this Work. This treatise though edited and a compilation is still way highly useful to even serious graduate students, researchers and Faculties in the area of Philosophical studies in Indian Universities. All those interested in seeing A regeneration of interest in Humanities in the face of obliteration threatened by Social and Managerial Studies in our times should welcome this publication.

Dharmendra Goel

Retd. Prof. & Head, Panjab University

Chandigarh (Panjab)

Introductory Note

A Note on Normative Ethics, Virtue-Ethics and Metaethics, and their inter-relationship

In order to understand the above topic it is necessary to understand first what is Ethics. Ethics is a discipline which prescribes rules for the conduct of human beings. It is only these beings for whom any rule of conduct can be prescribed. Such rules are the 'norms' according to which any human being ought to perform his or her action. Thus, Ethics is a *Normative Science.* Positive Sciences such as Chemistry, Physics, etc., are not normative, but are *descriptive.* So, they are not normative, but are *descriptive* or *positive sciences.*

What, then, is Virtue Ethics? Here one ought to understand, first the distinction between a '*rule*' and a '*disposition*'. A rule is formulated, but a disposition is either innate or acquired. In a sense, a rule is external but a disposition is internal. To illustrate, a legislative body can formulate a rule of action, say, 'while walking always keep left'. And this would be norm of behaviour in connection with walking. But, anger, kindness, envy, etc., are tendencies or dispositions which have their locus in a mind. Now, when such dispositions give rise to actions which are beneficial to humanity and/or entire existence, they are 'virtues', and when they are harmful, they are 'vices'. Many moralists would lay stress on virtues, rather than on norms in connection with the implementation of actions. So, their Ethics would be characterized as 'Virtue Ethics'.

But, over and above the aforesaid two types of Ethics, there is a third type which is called 'Metaethics'. The business of this third type of ethics is to examine the reasonableness or otherwise of the first and the second types. This third type, viz., Metaethics is, therefore, just a critique. Its only business is to critically examine the tenability or otherwise of both 'norms' and 'virtues'. I shall explain this point by giving two concrete examples, one for norm and another for virtue.

There was a norm, and at many places it still is that a child must be married in childhood itself. But after critical examination it has been established beyond doubt that child-marriage is a curse. So, norms, if necessary can very well be changed. Now, in the case of virtue I shall give an example from my own experience. At Oxford, one day returning home from the university library, I met a well-clad adult-healthy gentle man who begged me one shilling. I out of kindness gave him one shilling. And then the very same evening I narrated this event to my land lady. She at once rebuked me and told me that I committed a crime by helping that beggar. Such kindness are not at all beneficial for society. So, kindness in the above example is not a virtue, but a vice. Thus, it is clear that the concept of virtue is very much context-laden. No virtue is a virtue straightway. And it is *Metaethics* which decides when a so-called virtue can be regarded as a genuine virtue.

It should also be clear by now that all the three types of ethics mentioned above are very intimately related to one another.

N. Mishra
Tilka Manjhi Bhagalpur University,
Bhagalpur (Bihar)

From Editor's Desk

It is conventional among philosophers to formulate definitions of its branches that would satisfy you in understanding what is their nature. However, most of time a cut and dried definition fails to satisfy our purpose of nature—clarification of the branches of philosophy such as ethics, epistemology and so on because the said definitions do nothing but state some of the task of these branches, which remain either incomplete or scrappy, or else, the definitions are figurative or subjective exhortations of what should be done in ethics. Hence, the most important aspect of thorough clarification of "tasks" of the branches of philosophy remains neglected, which, however, should not be the case. It is desirable, therefore, that for the clarification of the nature of ethics or what ethics amounts to, we need to state what are "tasks" undertaken by ethics or moral philosophy.

A number of things are done under ethics, the most important being, the critique of ethical *language* or what call *"metaethics"*, the study of norm or bases of evaluation of voluntary human actions for their moral worth, which is known as "normative" ethics the study of moral values and virtues or "*Virtue ethics*", and the aspects of practicability of ethics in individual, social and professional life, which are, practical and *"professional"*, ethics. More than this, we speak of the *"descriptive"* and the *"empirical"* tasks of ethics, the former, more debatably takes up the task of description of the psychological basis the ethics, the latter deals in the empirical study of the individual and social interactions to collect data and analyse them to find out what are their moral repercussions. The field of ethics is ever growing, we need to be careful to study the extending tasks and include them as well. It may be troubling for some of us not to include environmental ethical, bioethical and some other tasks under ethics task because the value laden environmental, biological and some such issues call for practical resolution whether through application of standard norms of ethics or through social discourses.

After a cursory statement of the tasks of ethics, that gives us a fair idea of what ethics is or what ethics consists in, we need to clarify the tasks a little more so that the readers of this work nurture no confusion about what awaits them in the following four sections of the work. *Metaethics* is also called *second order* ethics, the *first order* being the 'normative' or, which is *standard* ethics. The second order task, *vis-à-vis* the first order task is so called as it *moves beyond (meta)* the traditional normative discussion or the discussion of the value, evaluation and criteria of evaluation of intended human actions that affect a number of beings and things either adversely or favourably and are thus judged to be either desirable or undesirable, good or bad, right or wrong, just or unjust, a duty or not a duty, an obligation or not an obligation, a responsibility or not so, that is whether the human actions have a "moral worth" or a "moral value", not simply a drab "practical" or "emotive value". In this sense, *metaethics* as a second order moral inquiry is not about moral worth of human actions, rather, inquires about the nature, meaning and truth of the statements of moral value or the moral judgements. In this sense, *metaethics* is as '*after inquiry*", an inquiry that turns not to be concerns of value and evaluation but the "*language of value and evaluation*", which is more basic to philosophical inquiry, says many. Apart from the conceptual and language clarification, *metaethics* taken interest in the basic *logic of proving and justifying* the norms of the standards of morality that has been advocated through the ages as monolithic and sacrasanct *ideals,* most notably in the names of *teleology* and *deontology,* having a wide range of varieties of these norms. *Metaethics* is thus an "after inquiry" that turns to argue why or why not certain ideals are based on either a weak logic or a stronger one.

Traditionally, ethics has been dealing with values and virtues, that is, it is concerned about the human values and virtues in particular, not about the general theory of values (or axiological thesis of values) because moral worth of human demand which decisions and actions are truly worthwhile or have a value. Among a number of the assumed values, are the "virtues" or "dispositions of character", again, not one but many. However, there has been long debates over the relative merits or pragmatics of these assumed values (including virtues). Nevertheless, broadly there are *aretaic* and *deontic* values and virtues, that is values and virtues of human character and duties, which always makes good cases of inculcation among humans truly so called. There has been a lot of hue and cry about the transcendental or *spiritual* values and virtues as well, as is the case with *social* or *community* values and virtues, and even in the cases of non-spiritual, and anti-spiritual values and virtues. There is a good debate about the replacement of normative theories by inculcation of values and virtues because the artificial following of a norm in life and its adoption for all sorts of moral evaluation is thought to be absurd and unpragmatic, Hence, the clarion call is to shun normative theories (which is a anti-theory stance) and thus embrace value and virtue inculcation among humans. However, many of us argue that a return to theory without begging a norm of norms is equally absurd because without norms, to call something a value and a virtue is impossible.

In the midst of the controversy, of late, grew parctical and professional ethics. In fact, the practical and professional ethical tasks were udertaken since a long time in ethics, but these fields grew in prominence and late as 1960s. There is a lot of confusion about what exactly is practical and professional ethics. Many ethicists thought that practical ethics, is nothing but ethicists' dynamic involvement in applying one or more ethical norms (as seen above) to resolve one or more practical problems which are also value-laden, that is, they raise distinct questions of moral worth or value. Similarly, professional ethics is nothing but resolution of professional value-crises by applying standard ethical rules and codes; of late, ethicists thought that apart from these dynamic concerns involving norms, ethicists should take up necessary theoretical inquiries as well, such as dealing with the modes of application, logic of normative application, weighing strengths of normative application and so on.

Professional ethics takes up theoretical inquiries about the nature analysis of profession, professionalism, ethics of a profession and ethics of professionalism. Interestingly, both practical and professional ethics came closer to meta-inquiries as nature analysis and logic of justification of these fields were urgently needed. Gradually, critiques of artificial or engineering model or application of norms by ethicists in resolving practical and professional problems paved way for new way for applied and professional ethics demanding involvement of ethicists, non-ethicists and those directly or indirectly involved in a value-crisis for resolution, in which not one or more theories are applied as mere tool or tools rather, in which spontaneity of moral opinions and arguments resolve crises, which, when analysed after a dialogue by ethicists, give us the norms of ethics which were dynamic or applied in a unique non-engineering manner.

Ethicists classify value crises troubling persons of occupations and professions needing resolution and their theoretical analysis as environmental, bio-medical, educational, economic, business, administrative, managerial, and social and political in the main, thus giving us environmental ethics. We also have engineering ethics, nursing ethics, war ethics, accounting ethics, financial ethics and many more.

This book takes utmost care to do justice to unravel the said tasks of ethics through the thirty seven papers that were contributed by authors of our times in India. It is testimony to the fillip that ethics has given to the Indian ethical diaspora. The essays are thus carefully arranged moving from the second order to the first order tasks of ethics, and then to virtue ethics.

The series on Ethics and Applied Ethics is a very ambitious multi-volume scheme and an outcome of painstaking and careful selection of papers contributed by the noted Indian writers on Ethics, which is as broad as covering the first and second order ethics, as well as virtue ethics, and practical and professional ethics. The selection and arrangement of the contributed papers was based on both merit and pragmatics, Special care has been taken to include papers concerning key issues and problems in the field of ethics.

Shiva Nath Prasad

Debashis Guha

Avinash Kumar Srivastava

Preface

The present multi-volume series "Ethics and Applied Ethics" is an ambitious enterprise and is intended to bring man, to the right rails of morality as the basic end of life, society, as also to wed morality, to all departments of knowledge, framed, created, and developed by man. Since all developments are for man, and man always aspires to be at the centre, so to devoid man of morality, would be nothing more than devouring the same man, who, being at the pivot of everything, development of all arts, science, crafts, knowledge, by his own hands through rational deliberation. Is this not great malady and a tragedy, indeed?

The present world is ridden with multitudinous crisis, i.e., crisis in the plural and the main anxiety of man in the recent scenario of moral destitution, is to end the crisis that has created an impasse or halt in several ways and man now is feeling suffocation of the worst kind. His heart - felt desired need is, naturally, to make all out efforts to resolve the crisis forthwith. But can it be possible? This is a question, which once tackled and solved, the other thing would be normalized naturally and bring a scope for peaceful sailing of life.

In this context, it would be essential to know the meaning and the content of the very word "crisis", which is eating into the vitals of every man, whether the common man on the street, or those who are enriched enough to avail all luxury. Fortunately, the word crisis is a good word and it is not incorrigible too. The word crisis has been defined as a "process of transformation", so to mean, crisis is not close-ended, but on the contrary, it is open-ended.

When crisis is not close ended, it would signify that crisis as process can be reversed in order to amend, if the very process is wrong, thus, by reversing the process, one can reach at the right point, rather than remain in the state of flux or helplessness. But who can reverse this process; it is only man, who can help himself. Man's omissions and errors can be amended, set right, or rectified by man himself.

In this context, it is essential to make a distinction between crisis and natural disaster, or natural calamity, like earthquake, tsunami, flood, etc. Natural disaster is caused by nature's fury or any supernatural causes, as it is commonly understood. But contrary to it, most of the crises are man's own making and what man has done, it can be amended by man alone, it is within man's capacity to either control the crisis, or remove it altogether for all time. But the tragedy is that, man has become confined in the cobweb which man himself has created, out of his venom, out of his own wilfulness, out of his devilish desire of discrimination, divisiveness, angularities and everything that is evil in him, lying dormant, every moment, goading man to behave in wrongful ways. The question then is, can man succeed in destroying the fetters of multitudinous crises like social, political, economic, psychological and technical and spate of others? The answer is a positive assertion of "YES", but how?

Earlier, it was believed that God created everything, to top it all, He created man as the crown of His creation and in His image, but having created man, he also made a provision for sin, owing to man's disobedience, in not eating the forbidden fruit. Thus God also created sin and disobedience too. He violated his own limitations and constraints. Man was created by God, but man out of his own mental capacities and imaginations, created the image/ photograph/ idol of God and God was fettered in his own creations, he became captive to his own made prisons of limitations. Man also created many things, many arts, artifacts, art, crafts, sciences, technologies, society, wealth and thousand of things, thousand types of knowledge, but the result was that he became captive to his own creations and now that he wants to set free, from his own cobwebs and cocoons. Man can free himself, provided he wills firmly, resolves firmly. All this involves a process, to develop faith, trust, reliance in himself, to change himself to bring a total regeneration by removing what are evil aspects in him, his needs, his limitations, his envy, jealousy, instincts and impulses, anguish and angularities, his wants, his hankerings, which are really captivating him and not giving a way for moral upliftment, to make him see every thing as divine, to take all as equal, brotherly, friendly and humanly. This is really a lack of moral sense, that is causing moral crisis, which is the mother of most of the crises, if not all. So by inculcating moral sense, man can rise to the level of perfection, often attributed to the Divinity. With the advancement of knowledge, there has been enlargement in the domain of ethics and ethics with its lots of theories have enriched its stock. The volumes to come would take up separate department of knowledge–sciences and try to examine how the crisis caused and crept therein, can be rectified by the touch of magic-wand of moral ideals, which have now come to the lowest ebb, or placed in a state of stupor and now, by ridding which man can create a new humanity on earth, a spiritual moral globalization, rather than bring about a consumerist culture of material globalization or global competitiveness, callousness, cold war, terrorism, fundamentalism, barriers to humanity, dividing man from man. If our efforts succeed even a little bit with the ethical discussion presented in these volumes, we will feel prized beyond all bounds and rewarded amply.

Shiva Nath Prasad
Debashis Guha
Avinash Kumar Srivastava

Acknowledgements

We acknowledge our deep sense of gratitude to all the scholars, who have taken pains to contribute their choicest papers, to the present volume, entitled "Issues in Metaethics, Normative Ethics and Virtue Ethics"; not only for submitting papers after deep deliberation, or for taking pains to write for us, but for the prime reason, that they had to wait for years to see their papers published. We have no words of apology commensurable to the ordeals of the great scholars, who have contributed their papers. Anyway, it is hoped that very soon they will have the book in their hands (as assured by the publisher) to console, "better late than never", but till then, we feel guilty. Once again, we humbly beg apology to all the scholars, as well as, our well-wishers, our elders, guardians, as also the youngsters, friends, relatives and all others, who have in any way, in any form, helped, cooperated us in this great academic adventure for bigger, valuable, pious missions and goals, at least.

We are thankful to Shri Shailesh Kumar Sinha, who very sincerely has computer-typed the manuscripts, correcting the print errors time and again, with extreme patience, as also with extreme sense of responsibility and humble meekness.

At the end, we express our sincere thanks to Shri Ashok Kumar Mittal, Proprietor of Concept Publishing Company Pvt. Ltd., New Delhi, who agreed to publish the series "Ethics and Applied Ethics" voluntarily, in the greater interest of academia, the researchers, Professors as well as, the general curious readers of the country and feel aware that Ethics is not only a part of university syllabi of Philosophy, but it is also an inseparable part of each and every man's practical life, as a key to safe sailing of life's boat, amidst the troubled waters of turmoil, discord, regrets and remorse, it teaches man, how to inculcate sense of contentment, rid of malice, avarice, scorn, hate and the like and to remain faithful, sincere, truthful friendly, sympathetic to all human beings of the world, since life is the precious gift, life is precious to all and sundry and no one has the right to disturb or harm anyone for one's own petty-interests. Man is born naked and dies open-fisted, with nothing to catch. So, the question is, "Why discord at all? Life is great, life is gigantic, a part and parcel of Divine spark. So, everyone is equal. Hence, the principle of "Live and Let Live", live peacefully and joyfully, is the key principle of Society and "Community". The word "community" "may be interpreted as" "common-unity", which is the guiding principle of "Ethics".

Shiva Nath Prasad
Debashis Guha
Avinash Kumar Srivastava

Contents

Part – I
METAETHICS

List of Contributors

Anamika— Presently, working in Deptt. of Philosophy, Kurukshetra University, Kurukshetra (P.G.) Deptt. was a student of the great scholar, Prof. Dharmendra Goel, of Panjab University, under whose able guidance, she completed her Ph.D. on the difficult subject 'Wittgenstein', also the same was published. She wrote several scholarly papers with clarity and consistency.

Bhatnagar, R.S.— Retd. Prof. of Rajasthan University, Jaipur. A most brilliant teacher, published several books in Hindi from Rajasthan Granth Academy and books in English, large numbers of papers presented in seminars. He may be contacted on 10/558, Manasarovar, Kaveri Path, Jaipur-302020, Rajasthan.

Chakravarty, D.K.— Retd. Head of the Deptt., of Philosophy, Guwahati University, Assam. An outstanding writer, brilliant teacher, specialised in Metaethics, presented about one hundred papers in different seminars—also a member of ICPR and committed academician.

Goel, Dharmendra—Retd. Prof. Deptt., of Philosophy Panjab University, Chandigarh, A Scholar of rare merit, known both nationally and internationally as a brilliant scholar, specialised in Western Philosophy, has written several books, reviews, attended lot of seminars, has more than one hundred research papers to his credit, no word of praise is enough for this rare genius. Contact 38 A, Swastik Vihar, Mansadebi Road, Panchkula, Haryana-134109.

Guha, Debashis— Previously, he was in Ranchi University, now

Prof. in Philosophy Deptt., Allahabad University (U.P.), also the editor of the volume; known nationally and internationally he has all through been serious in reading, writing, teaching. Seven volumes on ethics are the monumental works on ethics. More than hundred brilliant papers are to his credit.

Ghosh, Rituparna—She presented her paper, while she was a research Scholar, under Prof. Debashis Guha and later completed her Ph.D. Her writings are clear.

Ganguli, Pratima—Retd. Prof. in the Deptt. of Philosophy, "Bhagalpur University, a voracious writer, wrote several books of Ethics, in which she reserves her name, wrote very great number of research papers, very meritorious teacher. Now, she is living in Kolkata, with her son.

Kapoor, Veena— Prof. Deptt. of Philosophy, Panjab University, Chandigarh, she has specialised in Ethics. A reputed brilliant writer on almost all topics related to Ethics. Her writings are marked by extreme clarity of vision, contributed lot of papers in several Jounrals.

Mukherjee, Asha—Head of Philosophy Deptt. Viswabharti University, Shanti Niketan (W.B.) — a very well known scholar, known nationally and internationally. She has published several books, specialised in Ethics, above one hundred research papers are to her credit. Visited several countries of the world and lectured.

METAETHICS

Chapter – 1

Clarification of the Nature of Ethics

Rituparna Ghosh

If we want to have a sound view of the 'nature' of ethics, we should better avoid definitions assuming them to be absolutely true, because, a close look at the definitions reveal that they are all *partial statements* of the tasks of ethics. It is desirable, therefore, that we clearly state the different tasks of ethics to let people know about its nature and subject matter. Ethics does not have one task, that is, the normative task or at best another task that is the practical task, rather, it has many other tasks which needs clear statement now. Two things are to be noticed here, one is that, the tasks of ethics as has been revealed till date is phenomenal, and it is *growing*, everyday because we are finding important matters for *ethical scrutiny*, in many fields of study. Hence, the tasks as stated here need not be taken at absolute. Next, we have to keep in mind that with the elaboration of the various tasks of ethics, some of them emerge to be most important or critical, building the so called *structure* of ethics, which is of our immediate concern.

In our opinion, ethics is known for undertaking five important tasks, which according to us also constructs its superstructure. These are "the 'metaethical', 'the normative', 'the applied', 'the psychological', the 'analytic' and the 'virtue based' tasks of ethics. The order of the tasks as it appears here need not be taken as final. In many ethical traditions, as in the Indian ethical tradition, the tasks are arranged differently giving more stress on the 'psychological analytic task' and the 'virtue based task'.

It is difficult to imagine ethics without *metaethics* because the metaethical task is a considerable one in ethics. Without it the basic structure of ethics cannot be erected. At the outset it is important therefore, to explain what *metaethics* consists of or what are its tasks. Simply stated, the important considerations of *metaethics* is to unfold the nature, truth and meaning of *language of ethics*, and to analyze the different justifications available to us in order to logically establish the different norms for their acceptability. Clearly, discussion of the meaning or uses of the moral terms and utterances about the nature of the moral concepts should be termed as *metaethical* discussion. It is known by different norms. Some philosophers call it *'analytic ethics'*, or *'critical ethics'* or *'theoretical ethics'* or *'epistemological ethics'* or *the 'logic of ethics'*.

Avoiding the various terminologies, we can say that, *metaethics* deals with the logical and the semantic questions like, what are the meaning and uses of moral terms such as 'good' and 'right', etc., and what are the meaning and uses of moral judgements such as "truth telling is good", "helping the poor is right", etc. In one sense, then *metaethics* is concerned with the nature and functions of ethical terms and ethical judgements and, therefore, it is 'analytic' in nature. It has nothing to do with either evaluations of moral judgements or propounding the basis of moral judgements. Nonetheless, *metaethics* does take analytic interest in expounding the nature of moral evaluations, the inherent logic of moral evaluations and scrutinize the different justifications in favour of the different bases of moral evaluations. Frankena aptly explains, "*metaethics* does not propound any moral principles or goals for actions except possibly by implication; as such it consist entirely in philosophical analysis."[1] From this, we come to know that unlike normative ethics, *metaethics* does not have direct interest in finding out the standards of moral conduct, though it takes deep interest the justification of standards, of the logic of accepting ethical standards which are believed to be worthy of judgeing the morality of actions.

There is a conviction on the part of many philosophers that the *metaethical* task is the 'primary' task of the ethicists. Some of these philosophers argue that, it is the *only* task to be justifiably undertaken by the ethicist. These philosophers are mostly the logical positivists of the early period. We find such things in the early writings of Rudlof Carnap, A.J. Ayer, and Moritz Schlick, of the Vienna circle. The logical positivists thought that the task of philosophy and, therefore, of the philosophers does not consist in explaining things like ultimate reality and nature and creation of the world, to prove divine existence, etc. In fact, philosophy does not have any synthetic interest at all for it is different from the descriptive sciences, *metaphysics* and religion which deals with the above mentioned problems. Hence, the task of the philosophers is *analytic,* that is, philosophers should concentrate on logical analysis of the important philosophical concepts which constructs a gamut of philosophical language. A logical analysis of concepts of language thus amounts to the meaning analysis of the concepts and language. It also amounts to the truth of the different philosophical assertions. These thinkers, therefore, started maintaining that the most required and important criterion to determine the truth and meaning of philosophical language, which by virtue of Ayer's genius in particular is known as the *verification theory* of truth and meaning. Given this criterion and the task of philosophy, these thinkers argued that ethics as it has been traditionally understood makes little sense, because its primary task, that is, the normative task, is completely out of use because, to establish these norms is in no way the business of philosophers. If ethics makes any sense, it should be thus concerned with the analysis of the language of ethics and nothing else. In fact, given the verification theory of truth and meaning, the entire body of normative language turns out to be meaningless or nonsensical, which is also true of language of theology. Yet, these thinkers later on revised their opinions to accept that ethics as such, and ethical language in particular, is true and meaningful. However, ethics is sensible only if it undertakes this analytic task. Moreover, ethical language is true and meaningful only if it is taken as emotional utterances of the speaker. With this emotive theory of ethical language, comes to the fore, the theory that ethics is, or should be, pure *metaethics*. It is a matter of great concern though that the normative and practical tasks of ethics have been neglected by these thinkers. However, their opinion had inherent flaws, which often compelled them to make contradictory assertions Schlik himself in the work "The unity of science" asserted that what we call 'good' should be understood, for its meaning only in terms of utility which means that Schlik indirectly accepts the importance of utilitarianism as an ethical norm for determining what is good. Hence, his normative interest cannot be ruled out, though Carnap and Ayer did not make remarkable shifts in their ethical stance. The problems in accepting ethics as *metaethics* were prominent. One problem is that we like or not, the analysis of truth and meaning of normative language is the mainstay of the logical analyst. It is a matter of wonder what these analysts would do if the entire body of 'normative language' was non-existent! The analysis of the good, right, just, duty, obligation, responsibility, and many other concepts finds multifarious use in 'normative language' which needs to be analyzed for their meaning. These thinkers also forget that if we do not speak of *universalisible* principles in morality there would hardly be any basis of evaluation of humans as good and bad. If it is said that, evaluations of human actions are not the task of the philosophers, then the reasons should be clear, which, however is unknown to us. Why should not ethicists undertake such task, is unclear because, we cannot unilaterally declare something without giving satisfactory reasons like, philosophers *only task* is the analysis of language. There is no doubt that analytic task of philosophy is very old in the history of Indian and Western ethics. It is testimony to the fact that, analysis of ethical language has been considered as most important but, equally true is that the ethicists have been successfully and rightly trying to explain why certain evaluative assertions are to be accepted, that is, the grounds for accepting certain evaluations to be true . This is possible only if we consider that the normative task is most important. For example, analyzing the language, "truth telling is good" is not sufficient in ethics. We should ask on what basis we should say that truth telling is good and not bad. Finding answer to this is extremely important which comes within the purview of *normative ethics* which is there unavoidable. Again an interesting thing is that, if we "say truth telling is good", because truth telling has intrinsic value as being a duty of a person then, possibly we are following the deontological theory. Here, *metaethics* would come to ask why the deontological explanation should be taken as sound and not any other explanation? Hence, one of the most important tasks of *metaethics* which is to discuss the justification of the logic of the norms, tells us that *metaethics* is closely related to *normative ethics*. Hence, it would be utter mistake to maintain that ethics is *metaethics*. We will see shortly that *metaethics* is an important task in ethics and it is also closely related to practical ethics. We must not forget that modern *metaethics* does not necessarily accept the truth that it is nothing but analysis of language. Rather, it has another important task to perform which is the justification of the norms of ethics Clearly if we do not have discussion of norms of ethics, it will not be possible to perform metaethical task to justify these norms. It is due to this that the modern moral philosophers do not accept that ethics is only *metaethics*. On the basis of the discussion, therefore, we can say that truly, if some philosophers think that to call *metaethics* as ethics proper has regressed ethics as such, then there is some truth in it but most contemporary thinkers who believe that, *metaethics* is *one important task* of ethics among many tasks is true. As it is clearly reflected in these words "*Metaethics* is analysis at ethical language. It is very important and its ethical enquiry certainly leads mainly to two things: (a) The soundness of the logic of accepting ethical standards to be worthy of judging the morality of actions; and (b) The nature and function of ethical terms and ethical judgements".

From the discussion above it is now clear that ethics also includes normative ethics, which is sometimes called *first order ethics* as compared to *metaethics,* which is *second order*. However, first or second order really does not tell us strictly about real importance of the order of these tasks because we shall find that different tasks of ethics *together* constitutes the structure of ethics and, therefore, their isolated value or relative importance does not make much sense. However, it is undeniable that historically, normative discussions have been looked upon as extremely important and, therefore, sometimes referred to as *primary ethics* or *substantive ethics*. Substantive ethics as a branch of philosophy has been primarily concerned with the evaluation of voluntary human actions as right, wrong, good, etc., on the basis of some given axiomatic standards or norms which we have termed as normative ethics, as it is traditionally the most fundamental consideration in ethics. We call it *fundamental ethics* or *substantive ethics* for the same reason. The substantive ethical statements are of different kinds, for instance, we have actual moral statements like "You should be more helpful to others", which as suggestion or prescription tells us to do such and such things as they have been accepted as morally true. These statements often assume the role of an action guiding norms or rules of thumb. Yet, there are some more universal normative ethical statements which fill up the huge body of traditional ethical philosophy. For instance, "duty for the sake of duty is only desirable or good" and "maximization human happiness is only desirable end of life". It is clear, therefore, that normative ethics systematically tries to establish the general principles ascertaining right, wrong, good and evil, and in an attempt to produce such assertions, many important ethical questions are asked. Most important of them are, what is wrong? What is to be praised and blamed? What is desirable and undesirable? Hence, normative ethics or substantive ethics attempt at answering some fundamental questions in morality like what is good or right in particular cases and what is the basis of judging something as good and right. Clearly, normative ethics deals with the fundamental principles or standards of morality — their nature and kinds, and also about many *secondary* moral rules that follow from the basic principles. It also discusses about the ways in which such ethical standards are helpful in judging the morality of intentional human actions. *Normative ethics* thus provides us enough grounds for moral evaluations. If an old fashioned analyst sticks to the point that *normative ethics* is non-sensical then, there can be no moral standard. As such, all discussions historically done about moral merit, freedom, responsibility, obligation and duty become insignificant. It is, therefore, legitimate to assert that normative ethics is *within ethics*, and it is needless to argue that it is first order or it is most important. We have to remember that *metaethical* theories are about *metaethical* statements and, therefore, they are normatively neutral, but to think that there are no normative theories, would be a great mistake. The truth is that a moral philosopher should be involved with both *normative ethics* and *metaethics* and that they are in same sense closely related. We can say that both are inseparable parts of a whole called, 'ethics' having equal importance.

Normative ethics need not be simply conceived as empirical or historical enquiries of theories; it also does not make sweeping demands for particular normative or value judgements. It does not try to answer either particular or general questions about what are good, right, obligatory, etc. Rather, *normative ethics*, apart from other things we have mentioned, tries to answer important, logical, epistemological and semantical questions like, what is sense of morally right, good, etc.? How can ethical judgements be justified or can they be justified at all? What is the nature of morality? What is the distinction between moral and non-moral? What is the significance of freedom and responsibility? And how do we arrive at a set of acceptable judgements about moral obligation, moral values and non-moral values? In fact normative ethics is concerned with the classification of the general outlines of several normative theories to answer what is right or ought to be done.

In way of showing those how certain fundamental ethical statements are rationally supported, some ethicists became strictly *monolithic* that is these people adhere to one and only one rationally supported stand and to serve all the normative purposes maintained above. It is difficult to find dualism and pluralism in this regard, but the history of ethics which is ever-changing, is testimony to pluralism in normative thinking. It is not difficult in normative thinking to find some ethicists like Nietzsche, Camus and Marx who are critical of traditional normativism, which amounts to some kind of ethical skepticism. However, it will not be difficult to justify that ethical skepticism is itself a moral theory. It is also difficult to say that, ethical skepticism is anti-theory as well as anti-morality because, the above mentioned skeptics themselves had unique *theories* of morality and were in no sense anti-moral or immoral. There are also some normative thinkers like Kant and Sidgwick who are concerned with the fundamentals of *common sense* normative ethics but they are hardly anti-theoretic or anti-moral.

Contemporary ethics lays much importance to applied ethics. Application of ethics is not an alien idea in either early ethics or modern ethics. However, the way in which application of ethics has been widely discussed within the proper field of ethics in our times is distinctive because, many people have been concerned about present day moral valuelessness in societies. With much interest among philosophers and non-philosophers, applied ethics has become a serious matter to be considered within ethics. Yet, there is equally strong opposition among the philosophers about the relevance of including applied ethics within ethics. Such protests among the philosophers come from what we may call 'applied ethical skeptics', who are different from normative ethical skeptics in so far as they do not doubt about the importance of norms in ethics. Rather, they doubt on the application of ethical norms. We may say that, *applied ethical skepticism* is of *two kinds*: *one*-group of skeptics hold that applying a theory is a bad idea within ethics, because such things do not fall within the purview of philosophy, that is, philosophy as such (of which ethics is a part), has nothing to do with the resolution of the various value-laden practical problem. Such things should be better undertaken by the social reformers and not by the philosophers. Philosophers should be more concerned about *metaethical* tasks and at best normative task. We have seen that such opposition from the applied ethical skeptics is due to the logical positivist like Ayer and Carnap. I have said before, and I shall repeat that, performing these tasks do not clarify what ethics properly is even if it is granted that resolution of value laden problems should be undertaken only by the ethicists because ethicists may be one important party in applying ethics, but not the only party. Another group of applied ethical skeptics do not oppose applying ethics because it is not the task of philosophers, rather the opposite, for the reason that applying the standard norms of ethics like Deontology and Teleology cannot be applied to resolve several moral ethicists. The reason is that when our house is burning we cannot ponder over theories to apply them artificially. This criticism is strong enough because it has a half-truth inherent in it, that is, it rightly says that we cannot artificially apply any one or more ethical theories to resolve moral crisis. In fact many ethical thinkers like Kant, Sidgwick and even Mill had an idea that we can press into service either Deontology or Teleology in real life situations to come out of moral dilemma. But, we have to understand that, artificially even the best thinker cannot come out of all moral dilemmas by taking the help of any one moral theory, because soon there will be conflict among these theories. Unless we prove conclusively that only one theory is true, we cannot resolve all moral problems on the basis of a theory. Even if only one *theory* is true it will be impossible for us to show that all moral problems can be solved by that theory. This has been shown in our times by some applied ethical thinkers like Caplan, McIntyre, James Brown, Callahan and others. However, these thinkers like our skeptics did not reject the possibility of applying ethics because, there are different ways in which we can apply ethics, which is not the same as applying ethical theories. One such way is *intersubjective corroboration* as propounded by Debashis Guha and supported by others in different ways. Such application of ethics calls for *moral dialogues* among the concerned parties required to resolve a moral crisis through *corroboration of moral views*. Such an effort of applying ethics is, therefore, a united effort of ethicist and many common people because, all of us have moral authority to resolve moral problem by corroborating our moral views or our moral knowledge which we have gathered not by virtue of reading moral theories but by participating in the ecological community as concerned human beings. However, in *this effort* ethicists have a different role to play, which was completely mistaken by our skeptic friends. This is to select moral problems, arranging moral dialogues by inviting concerned people on the basis of well crafted morally oriented questions, guiding towards resolution, and most important, to perform a *post-corroboration task* which is specific to ethicists. This task is to analyze carefully and thoroughly the different moral views of the participants to show that so called moral theories are well reflected in the moral view of common people and, therefore, projecting the real dynamics of universal moral principles. If applied ethics is taken in this sense, there are no artificial application of moral theories though the standard theories known to us are well reflected in the moral opinions of the concerned persons participating in moral resolution. Ethicists take part in applied matters and do not remain mere theoreticians like pure metaethicists this way. We come to know that applied ethics is an important branch within ethics provided we accept the argument that, applying ethics is not artificial application of ethical theories by expert ethicists. It has also to be accepted that without conceiving the applied task of ethics, the ethical theories we have constructed are of little or no value because theories by themselves have no worth if they are not found to be useful in practical life. We also come to know that applying ethics is highly multi-disciplinary because in order to resolve moral problems ethicists have to take the help of several disciplines, like medicine, economics, management, environmental science and so on. If we keep this in mind, applying ethics comes closer to different occupations and professions as well because many practical problems of urgency are those of the professionals or people of different occupations. Interesting is to notice that ethics is a growing subject; its close relationship with different branches of knowledge is opening up new vistas of inquiry. It is due to this that today we speak about environmental ethics as an independent branch of ethics.

On the basis of what has been said thus far, we can easily show that normative, metaethical, and applied all the three tasks of ethics, which builds up its superstructure, are closely related as well as interdependent. The interdependence among normative, metaethical, and applied ethical tasks can be shown by taking the example of any value laden practical problem like *female infanticide*. We know that to kill female foetus is not only a problem in medical practice; it is an acute demographic problem in India if we go by the female sex ratio. As concerned citizens and ethical thinkers we cannot overlook this to do our bit by just saying, it is a practical problem for the doctors. In fact it is a *value laden practical problem*, which raise the questions of *moral desirability and rightness*. We cannot escape these moral questions and their resolution. Hence, applying *our* ethical knowledge is necessary, for which all concerned parties including ethicists have to work together. Once we do this, we come to know after the analysis of moral views that one or many moral theories are effective in decision making. Therefore, it is not difficult to see how and why normative theories are related to application of our ethical knowledge. Further; it is a matter of common sense that the *justification* of normative ethics and applied ethics as within ethics and the *justification* of the *model* of applying ethics are essentially metaethical in nature. Hence, normative ethics, applied ethics and metaethics all form a whole called 'ethics'.

We have to know further that ethics is not merely undertaking above mentioned three tasks because, the task of explaining the psychological basis of ethics is also very important. It is very important to remind that ethics is essentially '*agent focused*', and as such, we have to take care of the *purity* of the inner realm of the moral agent so as to find out the purity of the different factors enabling moral agent, such as to fix moral goals, means to achieve these goals through good intentions and motives. It is due to this that in traditional ethics we are concerned about the psychological factors such as desires, motives, intentions, determination and consequences of actions. Similarly, in ethics we speak about moral experience, moral knowledge, and moral sense as well as about moral exhortations, which are all known for their meaning only if we have some idea about the psychological factors underplaying in moral matters. The business of psychological ethics is also to explain about human conduct and character though it does not have any direct relevance to the judgements, justification and condemnation of the character and conduct. It is very clear that the psychological task within ethics cannot be to justify and condemn our actions, it is reasonable to hold that the psychological explanation of actions might influence our ethical judgements of actions. For example, the psychological explanation of a violent action does influence us to judge whether or not a violent action is good or bad and thereby to condemn our intentions as malicious or non-malicious. Equally important is to know that without *desires*, any sane individual does not intend to act. Without going through the psychological analysis of desires we cannot perhaps know the different tendencies of human nature on which the different desires depend on. It is due to this that we have to analyze certain tendencies of our nature like organic needs, instincts and general innate tendencies to know about our varied desire which lead us to intentional actions. Many psychologist hold that the sense of duty is one among many desires we have for our intentional actions. In fact, our acting from the sense of duty is often regarded as outstanding form of moral action whereas many others believe that our sense of a definite purpose guides our moral actions.

Ethics has been traditionally dealing with virtues and values, particularly ethical virtues and ethical values because basic human virtues and values are the basis of our ethical life. We have just seen that when we act and when we intend to act we should possess pure intentions, not malacious ones. Similarly, if we are not virtuous and care for values, we cannot be called ethical persons. Some people believe that as ethics cannot be merely theoretical but also practical it is equally important that ethics teaches us what are important values and virtues and how we became virtuous moral agents. In fact, these people believe that inculcation of basic human virtues and values are ethical in our moral life. Hence, it is not at all important to know about many ethical theories and the ways they can be applied in our practical life rather to become virtuous beings. In this way we have within ethics exclusive discussion on virtues which are now known as ethics of virtue or virtue ethics as different from ethics of norms or normative ethics. Sometimes, therefore, virtue ethics is considered as a revolution against traditional ethics, because it does not teach us what norms to apply and which theory to apply for value resolutions. Rather, it calls for the cultivation of certain dispositions and traits of characters such as honesty, kindness, conscientiousness, etc. These people argue that without certain traits of character, rather than traits of personality, there is no meaning of following principles like "duty for the sake of duty" or "pleasure for the sake of pleasure". The reason is that if we do not have any regard for dutifulness and purposefulness, that is, if we are not virtuous persons who are dutiful and purposive, any moral theory cannot make sense. Equally true is that if we do not have any regard for being benevolent, we cannot come together to apply our ethical knowledge to resolve moral problems. Hence, cultivation of virtues is crucial in ethics. However, many people point out that any cultivation of virtues like dutifulness beg a moral standard because how do we come to know that at this point of time we have become dutiful? Or, how do we come to know that at this point of time we have become purposive? People like W.K. Frankena points out that though ethics of virtue has an inherent truth in it, it cannot completely discard normative and applied ethics. Similarly, ethics cannot be simply concerned with the inculcation of virtues because it has to analyze the meaning of virtue and the different kinds of virtue such as benevolence, dutiful and so on. The consideration of the meaning analysis of virtue and different virtues is an important metaethical task which we cannot avoid in the name of pure virtue ethics. In this regard it has been maintained that a virtue is a *quality of character* or *a disposition* to do what is right in a particular situation or which universal duties should be performed. It is also said that a virtue is a *habit of action* which corresponds to the quality of character or disposition. In this sense honesty as a virtue of a man refers to the person's habitual state of mind to act honestly and as such corresponds to his quality of character, that is, an honest character. Frankena says, "A virtue is not a principle of this kind; it is a disposition, habit, quality or trait of the person or soul which an individual either has or seeks to have. Hence, I speak of the principles of beneficence and virtue of benevolence".[3] Frankena has further analyzed three important kinds of virtue ethics corresponding to the three kinds of ethics of duty, namely, *trait egoism*, *trait utilitarianism* and *trait deontology*. Under the first category there is an urge to encourage the virtue of personal welfare; under the second there is an urge to encourage social welfare; and under the last one there is an urge to encourage intrinsic moral virtues such as obedience, justice, etc. It has been said that inculcation of virtues need not be necessarily monastic rather pluralistic. In the modern times thinkers like Slote thinks that the ethics of virtue should be better classified as *agent centred, agent based*, *agent focused,* and *agent prior.* Whatever may be the controversy, the ethics of virtue in our times has been forcefully established by thinkers like Miss Anscombe, W.J. Prior and many others? These thinkers hold the history of Western ethics is a testimony to the fact that Ancient Greek ethics stressed much on a virtuous character rather than artificially applied ethical principles. This is more prominent in the writings of Socrates, Plato, and Aristotle. Ethics, therefore, has to elaborate on the different cardinal virtues as well as many moral and non-moral virtues which make it different in nature. Though there is no doubt that the growth of the ethics of virtue in the contemporary writings of Anscombe and others is largely anti-theoretic but many ethicists argue that virtue ethics need not be either anti-normative or anti-applicative. We have just said that, virtue ethics is closely related to metaethics because; we do need the clarification of the meaning of important concept of virtue ethics before we elaborate its nature. Similarly, a careful analysis reveals that the virtue ethics is closely related to normative and applied ethics, because the basic virtuous dispositions of a person is known to us clearly when we refer to certain theories. It is clear that if a person does not follow the universal principle of benevolence he or she cannot be said as having a benevolent character. Equally true is that if a person remains completely inactive and inert towards the several values laden practical problems in life, the person cannot be called virtuous. How can we inculcate the virtue of empathy or sympathy without acting empathetically or sympathetically? If we do not contribute in moral discourse positively to resolve value crisis, how can we be a moral person?

On the basis of the entire discourse, therefore, we come to know that ethics as branch of philosophy has a distinctive *structure*, which is erected by normative, metaethical, practical, professional, occupational, environmental, virtue ethical and psychological tasks. I would like to maintain that a *valid structure* of ethics should keep all these things in mind. If we say that any Greek or Indian thinkers builds an ethics it should have these components, but it is not necessary for any ethical writer to write about all these things at a point of time. It may well be that some ethical writers focus on the metaethical task and some on the normative tasks and some others on different other tasks. However, many brilliant writers of ethics often construct an ethics which reveals the said *valid structure*.

REFERENCES

1. Frankena, W. K. *Ethics*, Prentice Hall of India, New Delhi, 1989, p.95.
2. D. Guha, An enquiry into the Cases of Normative Ethics and Applied Ethics, *Journal of ICPR*, 2001, p. 21.
3. Frankena, W. K. *Ethics*, *op. cit.*, p. 64.

Chapter – 2

Epistemology and Ethics

Debashis Guha

A thorough reading and appreciation of the seminal paper by Richard B. Brandt in the third volume of the *Encyclopaedia of Philosophy* (Edited by Paul Edwards, 1974), titled "Parallel between Epistemology and Ethics" is worth considering because apart from other things it incites us to see the ways in which epistemology has something to offer in ethical considerations and the ways in which ethics has something to offer in epistemic considerations, though on face value (or rather based on myopic conception of tasks of epistemology and ethics), we think that something that concerns itself with nature, origin and limits of human knowledge has no concern with the one that concerns itself with matters pertaining to ethical value and evaluation. This chapter does not try to state what Brandt has stated nicely in terms of showing "parallels between" the above fields of philosophy, it attempts at showing that Brandt's ultimate finding that the overlapping areas of epistemology and ethics should be best seen (or rather exclusively seen) as cases of metaethical discussion wherein epistemic and ethical discursive elements mingle with ease, and thus the area should be called "metaepistemology"; notwithstanding, the confusion that it is not beyond epistemology or even beyond ethics, rather a fusion of fields called "*metaethics*" and "epistemology", other branches remaining the scapegoats. This is to say that in this chapter I shall argue that though "metaepistemology" might be a good music to our ears, epistemological considerations in ethics is far more wide and deep because epistemology is playing just as fine in normative, practical and virtue ethical discussions in ethics as it is in case of *metaethics*. Hence, relation between epistemology and ethics should be expounded by moving beyond the imagined parallels and overlapping of metaethics and epistemology.

Before coming to the central question whether ethics and epistemology are related only in terms of a fusion of *metaethics* and epistemology (or henceforth, metaepistemology), it is worth commending that "to find a few parallels" between ethical and epistemological *statements*, is not tantamount to a "reduction of epistemology to ethics" (or *vice versa*). Looking at the number of "parallels" between ethical and epistemological statements, some philosophers, such as R. M. Chisholm, say Brandt "reduces" epistemology to a "branch of ethics". Chisholm is so (over) enthusiastic because like metaphysicians he discovers a queer basis of epistemology in ethics. Hence, ontological status of ethics or queerness of the nature of ethics is that its statements *cover* all epistemic statements, or that, all epistemic statements are in reality or ontologically speaking, reducible to ethical statements. Brandt necessarily shows the inherent defects in such ontological thesis about nature of statements, but returns to his roots to argue that "parallels" between *what things are done* in epistemology and ethics is sufficient (logically) to justify that there is a queer ontological status enjoyed by "metaepistemology". But this is another story coming at a later stage. In any case, dealing with "parallels" between epistemology and ethics might lead us to either reductionism that epistemological statements are ethical statements; or, a finding that metaepistemology is a fusion of ethics and epistemology.

The former thesis (of Chisholm) is obviously fraught with many defects, the most glaring being confusion in the meaning analysis of statements whether epistemological or ethical; in Chisholm's case, the confusion is about the ethical. More problems are stored when such analysis not only finds a "parallel" rather, reduces one parallel thing to another the more basic one, thinking epistemology is a subsidiary or a "branch" of ethics. Chisholm thinks that *all* epistemological statements when analysed for their meaning amounts to complicated ethical statements because any assertion such as "*S* is *obliged* to believe in *h* than *i* reasonably" is *reducible* to another statement having the same meaning, that is, "*S* is *ethically obliged* to believe in *h* than *i*, if that belief is reasonable". Hence, a parallel in the meaning of epistemic statements and ethical statements enable us to claim that ethical statement is more basic (!) And that ethics involves epistemology or that the latter is its branch. Clearly, for Chisholm the *definition* of "obliged" is obscure and non-equivalent. In fact, both are not equivalent definitions in any case. Brandt rightly remarks that the sense of "obliged" has been obscured by a manipulation in analysis of meaning that is, adding "ethically" to "obliged" in the second definition which does not exist or is not logically implied at all. How can, "obliged to believe in what is reasonable" be analysed as "*ethically obliged* to believe in what is reasonable"? In what ways can both be equivalent? "Obliged" in the first statement (the epistemic) bears a *non-moral sense*, which in fact, conveys the sense that "we have an intellectual obligation not to be illogical or self-contradicting when we have enough reasons to believe in one thing rather than other thing or things". Whereas, "obliged" in the second statement (the ethical) bears a *moral sense*, which in fact, conveys the sense that "we have, apart from all intellectual and rational obligation to believe in what is most reasonable to believe, there is a serious moral obligation to remain steadfast in certain beliefs than become fools or bluffers". The second statement is a "statement of value" which brings out *unethicality* (that ought to be avoided) in cases of certain reasonable beliefs. The statement is really *not* about reasonable beliefs but about *the ethic of* being steadfast to a reasonable belief. Hence, the first statement is not an ethical prescriptive, neither is it an ethical evaluative statement because our "obligation" of being an intellectual non-foolishly prescribes at best a non-ethical course of action in life, which in case of abeyance may be cursed as "intellectually or rationally undesirable", but that is not the same as "ethically undesirable". If I deliberately choose to believe in *i* than *h*, even if I know well that reasonably the same cannot be done and should not be done, I am at best a "foolhardy", an "arrogantly illogical person", "a self-bluffer" and so on but by no extension can I be "unethical". One reason may be that many reasonable beliefs often turn out to be untruths and thus discarded. Hence, not always can an intellectual imperative be an absolute imperative or an ethical imperative. It may well be that "reasonable" beliefs thus do not logically imply a "moral course of action" though a "moral course of action" might imply that I have some "reasonable belief" about what "should be done". In this sense, the moral course of action that "I must be steadfast in abiding by palpable true beliefs" at least a *doubtful* true belief that I have, but a *palpable* true belief does not imply that "I must be morally steadfast in holding on to that belief". Quite often than not our clinging to true beliefs as moral duties amounts to scepticism and dogmatism because we tend to overlook that contrary truths are possible and that the fixity of beliefs is adverse to what is knowledge properly so-called.

We can now conclude the discussion to agree to what Brandt finds, that is, category confusion between the epistemological and the ethical leading to a queer ontological thesis should be avoided. We may add to this that a "parallel" between *some* epistemic and ethical statements do not imply that *all* epistemic and ethical statements are equivalent or that any of them are equivalent, and that even if ethical statements involve certain epistemic statements as seen above, logically speaking, there is neither equivalence between the two nor is there a primacy of the one (the ethical). In that case, more difficult is to imagine that epistemology is a "branch" of ethics for the reason that "definitions" of epistemological terms begs ethical terms. Hence, (over-)enthusiasm to equate ethics and epistemology should be carefully avoided. But does that take us to believe that "parallel" between "what things are done" in ethics and epistemology is reducible to the conception of "metaepistemology" as an ontological thesis of the mutual dependence of epistemology and ethics?

Answer to this question takes us to the position of Brandt as expressed in his essay. Brandt has some extremely strong reasons to justify that what things are done in epistemology *bears resemblance* with what we do in ethics. This is not strange because being family members of philosophy, it is quite likely that ethics and epistemology performs some such tasks which are testimony to their family resemblance. Hence, functions under ethics and epistemology having queer connection, connects them, though Brandt's use of "parallel" may be well taken as lines that never meet in actuality though they happily remain drawn on a plane. Truly, this is no less expected of ethics and epistemology because resemblances in functions does not logically guarantee equivalence (as seen above) or what we contend, an admixture or alloy of epistemology and ethics, that is, 'metaepistemology' because in that case the figurative of the "parallel" breaks down even if the case of "alloy" is not exactly an "equivalence". Without much squabble, we should first see why Brandt thinks that functions of ethics and epistemology implies their closeness as "parallels".

Brandt's basic contention is that both ethics and epistemology concerns themselves with "beliefs", the former is concerned with beliefs about ends and means of an active life of intention, decision and action; the value of human deliberations and actions; the standards of evaluation and the justification of the standards of evaluation. The latter is concerned with beliefs that "taken broadly to go beyond mere predilections of consequences of the use of certain means to include theories, explanations and system of mathematical thought".[1] There should be least hesitation in accepting that an extension of "belief" in the sense of Brandt leaves no room for scepticism about "ethical beliefs" being inclusive. Truly, any belief about the first principles of morality or the secondary cues are reasonably good theses about moral evaluation that stands tests for pertinence or logical strengths and weaknesses as does our common beliefs about entities, facts and the world. A note of caution is that despite the "resemblance", concerns about "beliefs" in morality and epistemology falls apart as lines that never meet for their category differences, that is, epistemology, without being involved in any ethical commitments or judgements (remaining *ethically neutral* so to say) scrutinizes "beliefs" that are ethical on grounds available to it, but ethics is necessarily involved as non-neutral in ethical matters and judges its beliefs or scrutinizes them on different grounds available to it. Hence, scrutinizing the belief in a utilitarian first principle, ethics refers necessarily to grounds such as, psychological nature of man to desire the desirable thing such as pleasure and the calculus of consequences of actions, whereas remaining 'neutral to' such grounds, epistemology might enquire into the status of the belief in a psychological justification of the principle or the calculus of consequences or the first principle itself to find out whether such beliefs are justified, true and uncontradicted. In this sense, though similarities or resemblance between ethics and epistemology holds good, they are nevertheless, "parallel" but not amalgamated or alloyed as a field unique in its own right. Though there is no doubt that the similarity between the two seen just now, 'transcends' (*meta*) the discussion of the normative first principle, its nature and kinds to enter into a "meta-discussion" or "the logic of the principle itself", it does not imply that for that matter we need to speak of "metaepistemology" because epistemology makes sense only when there is a "meta-study" in ethics. The moot point is to scrutinize the validity of the assertion of Brandt that: "epistemology is not reducible to ethics, there is still a parallel between the higher order questions and theories to which epistemology proper leads and those to which normative ethics lead. The dealing with these epistemological questions corresponding to the discipline of *metaethics* we may call *metaepistemology*. The central question of these disciplines roughly, is how the statements of normative ethics and epistemology proper respectively, can be supported what their "logic" is. The task of showing this is different, of course, from the task of producing a specific line of reasoning in support of specific ethical or epistemological principle".[2]

As we find now, Brandt is sure that metaepistemology is a 'meta-inquiry' covering both ethics and epistemology and are thus not merely "parallel" but "alloyed", because as a unique "discipline", he says, it has to take on the task of scrutinizing the "logic of ethical and epistemological statements". However, if we can show that without hopeless misadventure of both ethics and epistemology to enter into alien fields without a proper reason, there are enough reasons to find out ethics *contributing* to epistemology and *vice versa*, though much beyond the rigours of meta-study, there is first of all no reasons to conceive of a relation of ethics and epistemology by virtue of what both does with language, there is no reason to conceive of metaepistemology to explain what exactly should ethics and epistemology do if they are related. Going back to "what is done in normative ethics" one finds that statement of nature and justification of norms of standards of moral evaluation and the analysis of truth and meaning of normative language does not tell us the entire story of normative ethics because in it we are also concerned with "*following* the real prescriptions" or "a course of action" for a quality-of-life. Normative ethics has been perennially prescriptive and this bundle of ideals for an ideal life, which we *believe* to be of value or worth, of worth pursuing and thus believe that following it, is good for us for a qualitative life. We do follow them by choosing appropriate means. Normally then, we are at the receiving end of moral blame when what is believed to be reasonably justifiable to follow as an ideal of life is put in abeyance or the opposite is *done*. Hence, the concerns about 'real life' *beliefs* of real people, whether philosophers or others, about an end of life and course of action that is desirable, and the *ethic of doing what is a justified moral belief* is something that tells us why normative ethical discussion like this involving talk about epistemic issues like 'belief in ideals' are deeply related though they are beyond the jargon of language and logic. "The ethic of" doing what is believed to be morally desirable is an *aspect of life* that poses least troubles of language and logic for real life people, whether philosophers and non-philosophers. When empirical ethics studies cases of "believed as desirable" and "remaining neutral or not doing what is believed to be desirable" or "doing what is believed to be desirable", takes us to a study of real life people pursuing courses of action and the discovery of the "ethics of" believing and doing for an ideal life. These things in ethics as we understand in relation to epistemology makes interesting study, which is by no extension metaepistemological, yet ethics and epistemology are related deeply.

Coming closer to practical aspects of ethics and the discussion of value and virtue-basing between ethics and epistemology, there is no need to imagine the necessity of a meta-study. Without going into any scepticism about practical and virtue ethics, we find that these things are functions of ethics that involves epistemic beliefs but does not fall in the realm of a meta-study. The sense, in which practical ethics is understood today, is an enterprise that apart from other things it is concerned in the main in the pursuance of a quality-of-life and quality-of-work-life, *resolution* of value-laden practical problems through dialogue among concerned parties amounting to some kind of resolution.[4] Again the key to such enterprise (as in empirical ethics), is the real life involvement of people in a course of action that is closely related to *belief about* what is a desirable course of action in the face of moral dilemma, the belief about what should be done when some problems are resolved and decision-making rules are found, and what things are done in reality, amounting further to normative evaluations for moral blame or praise. This must be equally true in case of believing what things are ethically valuable and virtuous and what has been done or not done, again awaiting evaluative judgements. All these studies in ethics or all these tasks of ethics as they get related to the inquiry of our belief systems in real life, transcends the logic of justifications. Hence, ethics and epistemology are closely knit in many cases, that is, in cases of what things are done by them other than the analysis of language and logic. Conclusively, meta-study does not exclusively bind ethics and epistemology to construct an alloy of "metaepistemology". This, however, is also an assertion of the truth that despite language and logic making ways for epistemic and ethical reduction, transcending them also paves new ways to relate them.

REFERENCES

1. Brandt, Richard, "Parallels Between Epistemology and Ethics" in Edwards, Paul (eds.), *Encyclopaedia of Philosophy*, Vol. 3, MacMillan & The Free Press, London, 1974, p. 6.

2. *Ibid*., p. 7.
3. For a detailed study of empirical ethics it is suggested to go through the work of Ben Kimpel. *Principles of Moral Philosophy*, Philosophical Library, New York, 1974. This makes a good study for ethical and epistemological relation beyond the meta-study. Readers may also refer to my work: *The Primer of Applied Ethics*, Concept Publishing Company Pvt. Ltd., New Delhi, 2007.
4. For more details about practical ethics and virtue ethics, as well as, epistemological questions that emerge in this regard, readers may go through my work: *The Primer of Applied Ethics, Ibid.*

Chapter – 3

I know that Truth-telling is Good

Debashis Guha

"I know that truth-telling is good" is a complex statement having an apparent simplicity. It is two-rolled-in-one type of a statement; one part makes an *epistemic claim*, "I know", most likely by a moral agent and the other part making a *moral-value claim*, "that truth-telling is good" by the moral agent. Both these claims are obviously different owing to their intrinsic nature. On the one hand, we find an intentional human action has been evaluated for goodness, it is therefore, an evaluative statement as well, and on the other hand, we have an assertion, essentially non-evaluative in nature. When we look at the first part of the claim of the moral agent, which is epistemic in nature, it is obviously incomplete if treated in isolation. It does not tell us what the moral agent knows. Hence, "I know" is an incomplete assertion when uttered in isolation. But it does state that there is at least someone (the claimer "I") in the world who is in a state of "knowing" and that the person is making a claim of unique feature, that is, he or she "knows" something not beyond the world or not to be denoted in a natural spatial-temporal setting. Many enthusiastic epistemologists might be thinking about an isolated epistemic inquiry about "I know". Is it not true that we may inquire about the status or meaning of "I" and of "know" in "I know"? Is it not a sensible inquiry? Well, it may be an interesting inquiry and very easily enter into the realms of phenomenology, transcendentalism, metaphysicalism and queer objectification. Not only this, as already stated above, we may write pages about "know" in "I know". We may debate at length about the status of "know", as many books on epistemology have already done. But in this chapter, I am not at all concerned with knowing either the meaning of "I" or "know" or "I know" separately. Others may do it. Equally true is that in this chapter, I shall make no inquiry about the possibility of a transcendental/metaphysical/ psychological "I" and about "knowledge". Hence, any attempt at poking an epistemic nose to sniff the transcendental, etc. "I", "know" and "I know" will be a futile exercise. Similarly, when we come to isolate the assertion, "truth-telling is good" for its meaningfulness and suddenly start questioning about transcendental, etc. "Truth" with a dogmatic capital 'T' and about transcendental, etc. "Good" with a sacrosanct capital 'G', you seriously miss my point. So do not flog "an epistemic claim about moral value" to dance to your transcendental tune. Here, "truth-telling is good" has a clear reference to an evaluation of an intentional human action, nothing more, and "I know" is a bald epistemic assertion if isolated in a moral speaker-hearer situation, otherwise with "truth-telling is good" makes a completely meaningful assertion. Hence, the meaning of "I know that truth-telling is good" has to be understood as a whole, not in isolation. Yet, we must remember that "truth-telling is good", even if in isolation, is not as queerly meaningful as "I know" and we do discuss meaningfully about the truth and meaning of such universalized evaluative statement in metaethical literature.[1] But that is a different story because here we are inquiring about the meaning status of an "epistemic claim" about a "universalized claim" and not the meaning status of isolated evaluative assertion. I take up this issue in particular because in day-to-day life in situations of moral dialogues such assertions are oft uttered. However, the evaluative claim may be substituted by other evaluative claims, like, "killing is bad". Here, we have to notice that even if we standardize the evaluative part and make changes in the assertive character of the epistemic part, for instance, a substitution instance of "we know" or "everyone knows", we need different analytic treatment for meaningfulness of the substituted statement, "everyone knows that truth-telling is good" or "all of us know that killing is bad". It would be enough here if we concentrate on the whole claim of moral agents for its meaningfulness.

The moment we look at the complex assertion, "I know that truth-telling is good", we have a clear idea that the moral agent is rather sure that some human intentional action is of great worth or is good. But is it not true that we are not so sure, whether or not the moral agent is sure that such an evaluation holds good irrespective of place, time and contexts? We can never be sure about the surety extent of the epistemic claim about moral-value because here we are considering the whole assertion in isolation, and an isolated statement like this one does not reveal its status or its meaning fully to us, that is, to the readers or to the listeners until we are placed with the utterer (the moral agent) in a situation of dialogue. Rather, the truth is that, kept in isolation, the complex claim of the utterer is of a superimposing character because the epistemic claim of the moral agent has imposed vagueness on the evaluative part of the complex claim which has an inherent universalizable character. Hence, any universalizable judgement of moral value is veiled greatly for its universal nature in the context of considering a moral agent's utterance in complete isolation. However, the universal nature may be unveiled depending on the actual situation of dialogues. We may thus come to formulate a condition of meaningfulness of such assertion by saying that "a moral agent's epistemic claim about moral value" is *context-dependent* or *discourse-dependent*.[2]

If the moral utterer in a moral discourse context utters the above statement we have for us other problems to determine its meaning. Either the utterer has accepted that truth-telling is good for him now (he is sure) or that it is good for all times to come (he is sure) or that it is good for all for all times to come (he is sure). The most crucial problem towards determining the meaning in a discourse situation where any of the three alternatives mentioned above is considered is that the utterer or the assertor "is sure". He is sure is to say that he has an undefective justified true belief about truth-telling that only "good" may be predicated to it. Even if the assertor says that in this dialogue situation now he says that only "good" ought to be predicted to "truth-telling" because he has "undefective evident belief", we have to ask a how question. Greatest problem is that the utterer or the assertor of the statement has almost deliberately advanced an epistemic claim that a simple, non-natural and indefinable property "good" may be understood pertinently along with "truth-telling". May be the utterer have other ways to understand "good", which is not a primary problem here because the problem is why "truth-telling" makes a good case of understanding "good" and not otherwise. This is the real problem of the "I know" type of claim in this context. To put it simply now, "an epistemic claim of a moral agent about moral value considered for its meaning in a dialogue situation now or whenever asks for reasons of indubitability of the use of "good" with some definite moral descriptive such as "truth- telling".[3]

One reason of such "sureness" (let us use this simple term) of "truth-telling" is what is only good and not bad is that the moral agent has verified it (the fact of telling a truth) to be good or of worth. It may be that the moral agent was a testimony to verification or that he believes in someone's verification to be valid one. Whosoever has conducted the verification of telling a truth, the crux of the problem is how he could or she is sure about an absolute truth of verification? In other verifications, telling a truth may be found to be extremely bad. It is due to this that even if we do not define "good" but describe it only on the basis of truth-telling or we fix "good" to "truth-telling" we commit a blunder, which in Plato's terminology is "the fallacy of defining by identity". And to Moore it amounts to a "naturalistic fallacy" of equating non-natural good and naturally existing truth-telling. Moreover, it would be very interesting to see how exactly telling truth by virtue of an experiment or verification turns out to be good. Some people argue that in verification, we do not "see" that truth-telling is "good" rather; we see some beneficial consequences of telling a truth and thus "know" (be sure) that it has been verified as good. But any careful study of consequences of telling a truth by the moral agent or others in terms of "benefits" is to justify that "truth-telling is beneficial" and not "good" unless you have already stipulated the meaning of "good" in terms of "that which is beneficial". Interestingly, such fixity would amount to fixity of a normative claim that "only what is beneficial is good". It would be trickier to verify this sweeping universal normative claim either. Another interesting thing to be known is how on earth do we actually verify a case of "truth-telling" as beneficial. If there are definite ways to do so, why verification would not reveal unbeneficial cases of truth-telling? So "I know that truth-telling is good" poses a serious epistemic problem, it is the problem of accepting the justified true belief about moral valuations. It is due to this that (a) good is not a necessary predicate to truth-telling; (b) truth-telling is not necessarily known to be either good or bad in verification; (c) any consequence of truth-telling would not tell us about its goodness necessarily; (d) truth-telling cannot be an absolute description or definition of "good"; and (e) an epistemic claim about moral value cannot be purely cognitively supported either in isolation or in a dialogue situation.

Other pure cognitive way to understand the "surity" of the epistemic claim that "truth-telling" has to be "good" and not otherwise are those of innatism, *a priorism* and intuitionism. But all these cognitivistic ways of "sureness" have some defects. If someone thinks that at a moment of history when he or she had first told the truth or heard it, he or she was sure (knew) that it was "good" and nothing else because the knowledge of the goodness of truth-telling was there in mind's Pandora's box. So everything he knew is beyond doubt. And remember when he knew at other moments of his history that truth-telling at some practical situations were bad and not good, it was perfectly all right in his Pandora's Box. Do we accept this option? No, because in reality innateness is utter failure in explaining and also resolving the above mentioned conflicting or relative value claims with regard to a particular intentional action. Moreover, an actual or real-life epistemic claim of a moral agent for some definite moral-value depends largely on having an intricate moral life (which includes moral agreements and disagreements). Epistemic claims do not drop from the mental framework by virtue of something like Plato's Phaedo-type recurrence of wise souls.

The internalists have for us *a priori* and the intuitive to prove how an epistemic claim that only "truth-telling is good" holds well. Here, at the outset we have to keep in mind the above conflicting claim that "truth-telling is sometimes bad as well" because by virtue of immediate cognition if one claim is possible, the other should be equally possible. Such conflicts particularly within the realm of inter-personal evaluation situation pose serious problems to *a priorism* and intuitionism. We have to also understand that the sphere of moral claims have strong empirical anchor. Devoid of the world, actual people, real behaviour situations, lively dialogue conditions, agreements and disagreements, no amount of pure reason or intuitive faculties can help an epistemic claim like the one we are speaking about. Yet, one may argue that these empirical anchors are needed for an introduction of truth-telling, that is, an introduction of an action to our rational-intuitive inner framework and the claim "good" does need either pure reason or intuition. Otherwise, there can be no way to fix "good" to "truth-telling" in an epistemic assertion. And even in case of truth-telling being bad at times, the fixing of "badness" is also by virtue of the same pure rational-intuitive faculties. So mere factuality of truth-telling would be insufficient, the imputation of "good", "bad", etc., non-natural values need pure reason or intuition. Let us accept that both *a priori* and the intuitive are sufficient for an absolute judgement or for an axiomatically valid assertion. But the fact is that no moral agent or agents ever have axiomatically valid assertion in the name of "truth-telling is good" because other axiomatically valid assertion "truth-telling is bad at times" contradicts the earlier so-called axiomatically valid assertion. And we do keep this conflicting options open in case of a moral agent or moral agents. Hence, moral agents' axiomatically valid epistemic assertions about moral value may be in serious jeopardy even in an inter-personal dialogue situation. Naturally, moral value claims like this one should be differentiated from other queer claims because an epistemic claim about Soul or

God or queer entities are not to be confused with moral value claims. Moral value claims are rooted to the empirical world, which is also a world of intersubjective dialogue situations. So it has not to be compared to geometrical-formal-transcendental systems. So far as "good" as a non-natural property is concerned, we have to remember that an epistemic claim about something being good does not necessarily presuppose that the "something" is an embodiment of good because that objective value is extremely futile to stick to, a fact we have justified before. We have to keep in mind that here the speaker or the moral agent is using the value-term "good" or that he or she is evaluating in terms of good an intentional human action and nothing more. It is quite likely that this use of "good" or "that, which is of worth" may greatly change in dialogue situations.

It is here that one is reminded of the pure non-cognitivistic standpoint that the epistemic claim about the moral-value of truth-telling is nothing but a statement of either emotion or, a suggestion or, a prescription or whatever. However, to find out the meaning of such epistemic claim purely on the above mentioned non-cognitive basis is not out of danger either because the whole statement is unique amalgam of epistemic and moral-value claims, and to add to it, the moral-value claim is conjoined with a definite descriptive which with the use of "good" does not immediately reveal or clarify the sense in which it has been used, lest, the whole context of use within speaker-hearer situation is clear. Hence, "I know that truth-telling is good" is not a purely non-cognitively meaningful assertion. Equally true may be that to consider its meaning the descriptive, the emotive-prescriptive and the epistemic claim parts all have to be taken as crucial within a moral dialogue governed by unique rules of speech acts. Hence, it would be a little oversimplification to consider the meaningfulness of this assertion purely non-cognitively either.

But our analysis has given us some definite cues to speak about the meaningfulness of epistemic claim of a moral agent about moral value. We have to remember that the statement in consideration is meaningful in so far as it expresses an *epistemic blik* in terms of the surety element of "I know". It is a *commitment-expression* of the speaker within a dialogue situation that he or She does have some justified true belief irrespective of whether or not it has been objectively and/or subjectively verified to be undefective. The commitment or the *epistemic blik* of the speaker in a speech act situation does not make it irrational. In actual *blik* claims about moral value, what counts most is what *descriptive elements* are available to the speaker (in this case that of truth-telling) and what *evaluative elements* are available to him within the *form-of-life* he is in, and finally how the evaluative elements available to him is *functional* in an actual evaluative situation or situation of moral dialogue, which is predominantly of the nature of agreement-disagreement.

REFERENCES

1. In metaethical literature we have interesting discussion about the meaningfulness of universal moral claims in terms of cognitivism and non-cognitivism. The former draws meaningfulness of moral claims on the basis of cognition of moral agents either in terms of direct sense perception or sense-verification or in terms of intuitive perception. Non-cognitivism rejects such possibilities and draws meaningfulness of moral claims by looking either separately into the emotions, imperatives, prescriptives, and suggestions, etc., of the claimers or take the different functions in moral language to be important.
2. Context-dependence of moral claims is well known; we now have to take care of epistemic claim about moral values in the same way. It is here that "beyond non-cognitivism" is a natural shift. It is a shift well marked in the attempts of P.H. Nowell-Smith and J.L. Austin. C.L. Stevenson has been an initiator in this direction in so far as the agreement-disagreement context has been well marked by him.
3. C.L. Stevenson and others did notice the truth that unfolding the meaning of the descriptives are necessary in any value claim but the addition of the epistemic claim imposes some kind of *blik* so that the unique descriptive needs to be scrutinized for its appropriateness to be qualified by a non-natural good and not left sacrosanct.

Chapter – 4

Value of Moral Skepticism

Debashis Guha

We know that in some sense or the other the Marxists, the Existentialists and the Logical positivists are supporters of ethical or moral skepticism, that is, these schools of ethical thought in either a strong or a weak sense do support the idea that there are ample justifications to doubt about the traditional or archaic ethicality's normative, metaethical and practical functions. More clearly, these skeptics have enough reasons to doubt that ethics ought to undertake the task of laying down monolithic normative systems which are universally and absolutely true, and that such true ethical systems needs to be applied by ethicists to resolve value-laden problems of practical urgency. Moreover, there is ample doubt over finding out "value" as something fixed or absolute beyond our consciousness, as existing naturally or non-naturally and evaluations for ethical value or disvalue are fraught with many risks than one if fixity of ethical standards control moral evaluation. But these doubts are serious ones, having enough reasons, not instances of whims, which reasons are pretty simply to understand and, therefore, attractive.

The fact that search for monolithic normative system has been a long enigma is testimony to the value of normative skepticism. Did we not academically brickbat for centuries to justify that "this" is the "true" normative system? And did we not fail miserably in justifying the so-called "true norm" for our academic and practical purpose? Mind it; skepticism had nothing to do with the failure of normative ethics rather, the archaic system failed from within owing to intrinsic defects in logics. One such defect amounts to the unacceptable logic of "having one true system" for "all practical purposes" for "all times to come" and for "all human societies (future inclusive)". In fact, such "having", that is, an urge, want, or need for systems is more academically dubious than not because intellectual search for norms need not depend on intellectuals' desire-satisfaction. And we know that fixity of belief is one bad thing to have when we are attempting at establishing an axiomatic system because axiomatic systems do not depend on fixed beliefs rather on many other things, may be a strong intuition (who knows?). Surely, one's fixed belief or one's incredible want does not amount to establishing an axiomatic system like deontology or teleology. That this is not true is justified by having numerous norms in academic ethics and they all emerged owing to logic inherent in normative thinking, namely, dissatisfaction and disagreement with the given logic of one system justified being absolutely true. Hence, the logic based disagreements within academic normative thinking independent of our beliefs and wants, etc., paved way for *relative* normative truths and not absolute ones. This simple truth has been the contribution of ethical skepticism in the context of normative thinking. It may be argued that the monolithic systems may all be true without necessary presumed infighting as we imagine but that strengthens the case of doubting one true system and does dissolve the case. It may be argued further that all norms being prescriptive in nature may be true in their own merits, and a search for prescriptions is so poor. But that again supports the doubt of the skeptics that there is one ought judgement to be revered as absolutely true in morality. It has been shown in the thesis on Marxism and Existentialist ethics that a careful doubt about absolute norms is not to be immoral or devoid of morality rather, to show that one aspect of normative thinking is that we may conceive of many norms and not one, and that it would be illogical and unfair to judge morality and immorality on the basis of "one" norm. However, this does not take us to necessarily and sufficiently admit that beyond norms we have to accept class struggle as the basis of value-judgements or accept one non-normative-naturalistic or non-naturalistic or non-cognitivistic explanations. The value of skepticism thus does not lie in what is concludes but in what refutes, and even if we debate about what it concludes, we find that the core of skepticism is quite logical—though tragically, there is no one explanation even within skepticism which ought to be sacrosanctly accepted as absolute. It is due to this that moral skepticism has been shaped according to various excuses for not having a norm or norms in the names of relativism, subjectivism, non-cognitivism, anti-realism and so on.

Focusing on the value of moral skepticism in general, therefore, we may speak broadly of two such things, that it has moral value and that it has philosophical value. The first is true because moral skepticism most logically enables moral agents to an optional standpoint in case of moral commitment and thus remains catholic in spirit in such cases. The second is true because moral skepticism empowers moral philosophers to critically evaluate theories that aim at justifying morality and, therefore, remain secular in an atmosphere of monolithic obsession. In this sense moral skepticism does not make us believe that there is "no reason to be moral" rather, that there is "no reason to be moral in one particular basis". On the same ground, we are able to understand that moral skepticism does not argue that there is "no reason to say that we have moral experience or moral knowledge". The value of moral skepticism thus depends on its denial of archaic moral thinking and a tendency to confuse it with archaic epistemological skepticism.

With this general value of moral skepticism in mind we may find out the specific value of moral skepticism in justifying that in our societies we do adhere to some moral rule or code at different epochs and these rules are of worth and to be pursued but there is no need to have persons in our societies to cling to any one rule or standard because none of these have universalizability and absoluteness. May be in different epochs, persons in our societies may justify one or some of the rules as of great worth but they may never agree to provide a universalizable reason or justification of the rules or standards of some worth at least. Hence, the value of moral skepticism lies in clearly escaping the trap of why I/we should be moral because any answer would amount to unjustifiable universalized justification or reason. It is better to have some reason but not thinking that it would go so far as to uphold why such and such basis ought to be accepted to show why I/we should be moral. So, we need not foolishly think that moral skepticism banishes a world where universal standards emerge or are clinged to with fervour rather, holds that it is a continuous human malady to cling to universal standards. David Copp succinctly puts: "the skeptics hold that no moral standard as such has an adequate and appropriate justification, yet she holds that subscription to a moral standard is an option even for a skeptic".[1] In "The View from Nowhere", Thomas Nagel holds that "most of the things we pursue are optional. Their value to us depends on our individual aims, projects and concerns. . . . they acquire value only because the interest we develop in them".[2]

It is thus a reminder to moral thinkers that moral skepticism is neither immoral nor anti-moral rather, have moral views or preferences in life like friendship or violence, and that the person may show unhidden moral attitudes towards homosexuality or heterosexuality. A moral skeptic may be thus at different epochs in societies have reservations about morally right, wrong, duty, justice and so on for that reason cannot be deemed to be anti-moral or immoral or amoral. Thus, "moral" will have perfect sense within "skepticism" and "moral" will have no necessary and sufficient dependence on archaic universal standards.

The value of moral skepticism may be evaluated by considering two questions normally raised against its claims stated above. One is that moral skepticism is based on "external" element or elements which are truly beyond the realm of morality as is the case with the economic and other excuses discussed whereas its basis ought to be "internal to morality", which has been supported by P.F. Strawson. The other question raised is that moral skepticism leads to "normative nihilism" as it shuts door for all normative and evaluative standards. Yet, both questions may be replied with success. First, by saying that a moral skeptic bases its justification on something beyond the moral realm so-called is to avoid circularity and question begging. Why violence at some epoch in society is morally desirable really depends crucially on the given epoch, the social conditions, etc., which are thus unavoidable for justification, and to call it "something beyond the realm of the moral" will be a complete misunderstanding of the so-called "realm". What pertains to morality of violence can never be some oversimplistic archaic standard or standards like deontology and teleology because these will miserably overlook the crux of the issue, the society in which at "this" epoch we are considering the case of the ethic of violence and, therefore, the factor does make importance within the morality and not outside it. Remarkable point is that doing infatuationless duty and/or an action with a purpose, can never be isolated from the real social contexts, the social tensions, changes and so on. So, there is no point in making a belligerence between "internalism" and "externalism". Otherwise when pressed upon for justification of the ethic of violence, we will square on to 'duty for duty' and for its justification from within, we either move in a circle to cite a case of violence as a categorical instance of duty or take refuge to an intuition. In the latter case, the easiest point is to remind that moral skeptics do have an intuition but it works only when we have considered the objective elements in the dynamic social milieu. From this, we come to know the "value" of an objective intuition on which moral skepticism relies and the value of transcendence of the realm of archaic standards to consideration of other things pertaining to morality. This point is crucial in realizing the value of transcending standards in ethical application. We shall come to it later on.

Now, let us reply to the charge of moral nihilism or better said, normative nihilism. It has been charged that moral skepticism is a move from completely shutting out archaic moral norms to some kind of universal skepticism that there may be no talk of rules, codes, and standards in morality as such. The point is that if this be true, any talk of rules, codes, standards which moral skeptics themselves refer to should be impossible and thus universal skepticism would defeat its case. However, a reply to impute nihilism in this case would be reminding critics that a moral skeptic does never attempt at shutting out completely all norms, rules, codes, etc., because at different epochs it does refer to social codes of wide range. So, there is no universal skepticism with regard to codes, what moral skepticism tries to shut down is possibility of having an overreaching norm as universal. David Copp aptly upholds the value of such skepticism as: "moral skepticism is more challenging and interesting if it is taken to be a restricted form of skepticism, which questions morality without questioning the credibility of epistemic standards and standards of rational choice".[3]

Given such support to moral skepticism and focusing its value in rejecting universally applicable norms in morality one comes to applied ethical skepticism. I have been trying to justify at different places that contemporary skepticism towards applying ethics is owing to a mischievous understanding of artificial application of archaic ethics to practical cases. However, equally worth mentioning is the value to be skeptical about the impossibility of applying ethics. Hence, if contemporary applied ethical skepticism is to reject artificial dynamics of archaic morality by ethicists and such trained coterie, then such skepticism does have a value in so far as proper methodology of application of ethics would be made possible by such a negative effort. We come to know that being skeptical about ethical engineering is to come closer to acceptance of intersubjective corroboration in which the common ethical dialogue concerns value-laden practical issues, its resolution, codification of professional decision-making and academic ethical post-corroborative analysis revealing real dynamics of ethical standards. And everything happens within the social milieu where people are deeply influenced by several "external" factors influencing moral decision-making. In this context fixity of belief regarding norms does not work much. However, we need not imagine that being skeptical about application of archaic standards amounts to application of moral dogmas but not ethics. In fact, what pertains to ethics has been made an enigma by academic thinkers quite unnecessarily. We have considered this point but another look at it will help us here. The moral experience all sane grown-up people have in our societies are experience pertaining to morality or ethicality meaning thereby experiences pertaining to what ought to be done, what is of worth, what is desirable, etc., within the given social, economic, political, religious, metaphysical and the ecological structure of the societies. This does not amount to what people of our societies nurture as dogmas of morality because many dogmas are constantly challenged and changed. They grow up or fizzle out completely owing to the moral or ethical proddings, most commonly not in isolation but in collection. Hence, a critical query of moral dogmas is functionality inherent in people's ethics or which is the true nature of application of ethics. Such application is not doubted in moral skepticism because it has a value of making ethics more functional, more dynamic than treating it a handmaid of ethical engineers.

When we come to "metaethical skepticism", we are clearer about the value of moral skepticism. When moral skepticism is in the form of metaethical skepticism, we have seen that it doubts the cognitive meaningfulness of moral assertions and value assertions. The cognitivity question has been the crucial one in metaethical skepticism. The point is not that metaethical skeptics has been great in so far as they rejected successfully the cognitive basis of the truth and meaning of moral assertions rather, they have successfully shown that moral assertions are not merely cognitively meaningful assertions for they are meaningful to us in terms of various uses, non-cognitive uses being extremely important among them. And herein one knows the value of the emotive, the persuasive, the prescriptive and the Janus-headed, use of moral language. Is it "is not an extremely important and interesting finding of moral skepticism"? Did it not help us in delving deep into the language discourse in morality to find out the cognitive and the non-cognitive status of such language? It did have a value in history of ethical studies and contributed greatly in our understanding of the performatives of ethical language by transcending the archaic patterns of intuitive ethics.

Coming to the question of "value-skepticism", we find more contributions from skepticism. The seminal piece of J. L. Mackie "There are no objective values" may be singled out to know about this contribution.[4] What has been most importantly projected by Mackie is that ethical skepticism in the context of value-discussion may be conceived either as first order skepticism in terms of meaningfulness of value-discussion (including all ethical values) or second order skepticism in terms of the meaninglessness of harping on objective values as existents in this world. More interestingly, Mackie declares that the first order skepticism is not skepticism in the true spirit, it is rather valuelessly negative. We thus come to know that value-skepticism is not becoming valueless or ethicsless or immoral or amoral. Rather, value-skepticism is a systemic, logical venture to discard the possibility of all archaic, absolute values (including ethical values) as some queer entities[5] as is the case with queer metaphysical entities. The challenge or skeptical challenge of Mackie and many others led us to consider seriously the cases of ethical relativism and subjectivity of values, which may have many defects but have contributed in compelling us to make a shift from our old, archaic moral thinking. We now consider the fallacies seriously in declaring some values as sacrosanct in this changing times and changing societies.

I finally cite two instances to justify that it would be extremely difficult for us to pooh! pooh! moral skepticism. Gilbert Harmanns points out that: "I see no knockdown argument for either side. A question of judgement is involved, "which view is more plausible, all things considered?" To me, the relativistic naturalist position seems more plausible. I have not tried to show that one side is correct. I have tried to bring out the central issues".[6] And this "central issue" says Phillipa Foot is "that we are all at sea with some of the ideas that we are bound to employ in any real discussion to divergent moralities. What we tend to do is to ignore these ideas, and pretend that the debate can be carried on in other terms?"[7] So, I conclude saying that it is quite repugnant to ignore these modern skeptical ideas because it steals the worth of several contributions such ideas have already made, and really there is hardly a "knockdown argument" against moral skepticism.

REFERENCES

1. Copp, David, *Philosophical Studies*, Ed. Keith Lehrer, Kluwer, London, Vol. 62, No.3, 1991, p.207.
2. Nagel, Thomas, *The View from Nowhere*, O.U.P., NY, 1986, p. 168.
3. Copp, David, *op. cit.* p. 214.
4. Mackie, J.L., '*Ethics: Inventing Right and Wrong*', Penguin, England, 1977.
5. *Ibid.*, pp. 38-42.
6. Moser, Paul K. and Carson, T. I. (eds.), *Moral Relativism: A Reader*, O.U.P. N.Y., 2001, p. 183.
7. *Ibid.*, p. 197.

Chapter – 5

On Logic and Ethical Justification

Debashis Guha

In the common parlance, logic and ethics are considered as sister concerns in the philosophical enterprise because both have among other likeness, the interest in what "ought to be the case", the former taking up what ought to be the valid ways of deriving truths from some given premises whereas the latter taking up what ought to be the just ways of intending and acting in the social milieu. In the extremely primitive sense of logic and ethics, the sisters are closer as "normative" enterprises within philosophy, each distancing itself by virtue of their specific goals or objectives. However, things are not so simple as they appear here because ethics is far from being a mere "normative" discipline, and logic is far from being a drab study of rules of deduction and induction. The point of concern here, that is, to analyse whether logic and ethics are related (and unrelated) in some ways would take us to believe that both cannot be seen as body of norms or rules which is so good to follow and nothing else is in store, for the obvious reason that the unfolding of the bearings of logic on ethics or the ways in which ethics opens vistas for logic, and that logic is so wide to enter ethical discussions, is something beyond a normative study, it may be a "metastudy", nevertheless. This chapter elaborates on the necessary aspects of the "metastudy" so that affinity of logic and ethics could be widely unravelled.

The "metastudy" demands on our part to elaborate on three

distinct but closely related matters, such as, (a) logical proving and justification of norms of ethics; (b) the nature and status of ethical arguments; and (c) the nature and status of ethical reasoning. In fact, an elaboration of logical proving and justification throws ample light on the two other aspects of bearings of logic on ethics, though some care must be taken in the two other cases. Interestingly, all of them moves beyond the boring study of norms of logic and ethics and still remains well connected as sisters in philosophical concern. A little care about the first matter in consideration would lead us to see that logical proving and justification are different matters or else the 'and' should have been logically replaced by an 'or', which however, is illogical because 'proving' and 'justification' are not one and the same thing in logic, and when we come to their respective roles in ethics, they must be treated as essentially different. This must be then an important logical starter to differentiate between 'logical proving' and 'logical justification', and 'logical proving in ethics' (that is, in normative ethics) and 'logical justification in ethics' (again, in normative ethics). Such an understanding of basic distinctions of the above shows us the sense in which logic and ethics remains close though different, and most interesting is that this comes to us as a "metastudy" not the primitive "normative" study.

Though logical proving and justification remain overlapped, very hard to dislodge them, logical proving nevertheless, carries with it the sense of "derived from", whereas logical justification conveys the sense of "justify to" or "pursue to". Yet, there are reasons to say that to "justify to" see a truth involves to "derive from" premises to do so, or, a derivation from premises is pointless without a concurrent persuasion to see a truth. Nevertheless, both may be involved with each other in this way but that does not logically enable us to derive and to see that, therefore, both are one and the same. Many related things are not necessarily and sufficiently synonymous. Logically, logical proving and justification are *not* synonymous — they are *not* logically equivalent either. This wisdom comes to us from many important sources, one being an excellent work by John Ladd's *The Logic of Moral*

Discourse (1957), where he distinguishes by virtue of some ancient wisdom provided by Aristotle that "*the logic of ethical discourse*" is different from "*the rhetoric of ethical discourse*" because basically "logic of" or "proving" is different from "rhetoric of" or "justification".[1] In this sense, "logical proving" as distinct from "logical justification" deals in the nature and role of standards *norms* or *rules* of deductive and inductive logic to see whether a *conclusion* follows legitimately from the *reasons* given in premises, whereas "logical justification" deals in the nature and the said role of the *reasons along with the conclusion* in the context of *pursuance* of the listener or reader of the same in real life. Hence, "logical proving" concerns with the *entailment* of the conclusion based on premises, whereas "logical justification" concerns with the *acceptance* of the entailment by speakers or listeners, *not* exactly on subjective grounds or whims but as based on counter logic or entailment that outwits the *logical strengths* of the former entailment or exposes the *logical weaknesses* of the same because it may well be that in an entailment premises failed to entail a conclusion owing to fictitious or unacceptable premises or that the formal rules were not followed. Hence, *not* all logical provings are acceptable or persuasive, and for that matter, they are not logically (necessarily and sufficiently) justificatory or that they logically justify some truth to someone. In this sense, though premises entail a truth, they may not justify the truth. The bone of contention in any logical proving, therefore, is whether premises and conclusion have a strong logical relation or formal relation because that should at least be acceptable by us for its obvious logical strength. Or, else, unacceptability becomes crucial in any logical justification because premises and conclusion fail to do what it should do when proving sways from the bounds of formality to reality to "prove a point to us". This must be equally crucial in the ethical context when a number of ethical discourse either fails to prove a point or fails to move an agent. Hopefully, ethics-talk is not illogical and non-logical, and for that reason, it involves "logic", when something is "proved" and when something is "justified". In the vast gamut of "normative" and "virtue" or "value" related *talks* in ethics, the basic *functional* or *dynamic* affair, that is, ethics-talk, which involves moral agents as speakers and hearers, who agree, disagree and debate continuously, involves logical proving and justification (or what Aristotle in his own way called, 'rhetoric'). The ethical discourses about norms, values, virtues and practicability, or application thus involve on the one hand the investigations of the conditions of proving certain truths and on the other hand, investigation of the conditions of persuasive élan of the truths in an atmosphere of ethics-talk. The former, we call, "proving" in ethics and the latter, "justification" in ethics, both forming the "logic of ethical discourse". Such "logic of ethical discourse" reminds us of what exactly we are trying to do here, that is, to show why and how logic and ethics, as different branches of philosophy, nevertheless, involve each other. However, before we move deeper into the territory of the "logic of ethics", proving and justification therein remains as distinct as in logic because in any case in ethics, proving concerns premises whereas justification concerns speakers of what is proved. Further, even in ethics (as in logic), justification is not "mere persuasion" such as propagandist or tactical pressure or subjective predilection (and, therefore, not exactly the Aristotelian rhetoric) rather reasonable offerings in favour of what is justified for acceptance, thus making proving its *necessary condition* though *not* the sufficient one because the acceptance does rely on some other factors such as the élan of the speaker, the awareness of the hearer and even the rationality of the hearer which is always at stake. Finally, though in the ethical atmosphere, logical proving may be *conditional* because even if the formal structure in valid, premises may *not* be true or acceptable, in the same atmosphere, logical justification may be *categorical* because premises have been ably pushed through outwitting the reasonable or logical challengers or hearers or there is no challenge at all. (In this sense, it may be closer to the Aristotelian rhetorical sense of 'justification'). It is, however, undesirable that the rhetoric outwits logic or formality and truth conditions of premises and, therefore, logical justification remains an *extensive* concept than logical proving, and that must be true in case of ethics-talk as well.

Hence, ethical justifications are more inclusive than ethical proving because apart from "acceptance", *grounds* for acceptance, that is, formal rules, acceptable premises and other conditions of acceptance are vital. This leaves no room for an illogical and non-logical justification in ethics. To harp again, logic and ethics are bound tightly for many reasons.

In an ethical discourse, therefore, *moral arguments* must involve concerns about premises, their truths, the formal validity and the entailment aspects of conclusion (which is another premise). 'Moral arguments' taken as a whole must then involve logic of proving and logic of justification, because moral arguments cannot be without a *purpose* in real life situations, though the aspects of formality and proving may be seen as beyond real life situations. Consideration of moral arguments thus takes us to the *second* aspect of this chapter, that is, the second metastudy whereby relation between logic and ethics is well explained. The basic point in "moral argument" is much like what Ladd has emphasized and R.M. Hare has dittoed in another way, that is, there must be "rationality of moral discourse". Moral discourse (the sense explained before), which essentially puts moral agents in the dock, if they are either non-logical or illogical (as seen before), must, therefore, abide by "giving reasons" which are often shaped as moral arguments when uttered about why such and such things are good and right or bad or unjust. Or, why something is a value or has a value. Or, why are something a virtue or have a virtue. Or, why certain practical decisions are ethically grounded or not. The obvious point is that moral arguments cannot be merely rhetorical without being logically grounded. Philippa Foot in her essay, *Moral Argument* (1958) thus emphasises that "The fact that moral judgements need defence seems to distinguish the impact of one man's moral views upon others from mere persuasion or coercion, and the judgements themselves from mere expressions of likes and dislikes".[2] Clearly, when it is said that moral arguments proves premises and justify something that has been deemed acceptable, the argument as such is functional in order to justify that certain "moral judgements" need to be accepted by hearers because the moral judgement or the moral premises is proved logically. Hence, moral arguments concern them to moral judgements of various types, most important ones being the *judgements as moral values and virtues* and the judgements as moral theories and/or principles or simply, *judgements as evaluational bases*. For simplicity in discussion, let us classify them as "value-judgements" and "evaluative judgements". There are then two aspects regarding these judgements, one is whether there are or there can at all be any formal logical proof to establish that these judgements are true, and whether, if they are true, they need to be accepted or they are justified and thus taken up seriously. Or, alternately can we say that these judgements beg no strict logical proof and thus justification, they are rather matters of either factual verification or they are simply based on heuristic understanding? More stimulating is to inquire whether such judgements can at all be justified by any formal or non-formal arguments or proofs or whatever because *per se* any moral argument and thus any moral judgement that has been justified obviously "breaks down" because available counter arguments and counter judgements necessarily do not prove anything than an absolutist stance of acceptance. In fact, the questions regarding moral arguments takes us to the question of *justification* of these arguments when "justification" is taken in its broader connotation (as above), which naturally involves questions of proving. All three questions are hotly debated in ethics, showing how long and how far we have gone in matters pertaining to logic and ethics, though I fear fool-proof answers have not been found. The scheme of this chapter does not demand that I state main contesting views in these regards rather to show that any attempt at answering them involves us in what we may say, "logic of ethical discourse", which is so important for Ladd, Foot, Hare and a number of ethicists. However, when we consider these three sets of inquiries about moral arguments, the last one is most challenging because it tends to be "sceptical" about any type of moral argument and thus moral justification, whereas the first and the second questions are "qualified sceptical" ones that raise doubts over "strict logical proofs and justifications" and the "scientific mode in proving and justification", the former banking mainly on deductive-inductive scheme of thought whenever it comes to ethical justification, whereas the latter relying mainly on scientific scheme of thought in the same regard.

Without involving into any details, we can say that those relying on "strict logical ways of thinking" in ethical justification are said to be the proponents of either derivations of "ought" from "is" or "is" from "ought", that is, the inductive and the deductive ways of justification respectively. The point is that the inductive way of ethical justification harps on "facts" as necessary and sufficient grounds for justifying statements of values and evaluation or value and evaluative judgements, which has been enthusiastically supported by the *definists, naturalists* and the *metaphysical moralists*, the former holding that ethical judgements (of two kinds as said above) are in fact definist statements of value terms, which are non-ethically anchored or factually anchored, and as such, such definist statements of value are logically contingent on non-ethical statements. Ethicist like R.B. Perry in the *Realms of Value* (1954) holds such a position. The "naturalists" on the other hand (much like the definists) need not necessarily hold that ethical judgements are statements of definitions of value terms; they are judgements derived logically on *natural statements*. Hence, ethical judgements are derived from logical arguments for which non-ethical statements taken as true or proved as true are needed. Most ethical egoists and hedonists are naturalists. The metaphysical moralists hold that statements of value and evaluation are logically contingent on metaphysical truths or statements embodying metaphysical truths. The theological and spiritual moralists are of such opinion. There has been heated debates about why such inductive ways of deriving "ought" from "is" should be done away with for bad logic. The badness lies in the *confusion of categories*, that is, to forget that ethical statements belonging to one category is not logically contingent on another category which has nothing to do with it because even common sense logic asks us to derive a premise if and only if its family member, at least one, is presumed to be true. Hence, on the basis of one or more non-ethical premise or premises, no ethical premise can be and should be logically derived. This must be true of all the three forms of inductive logical derivation, thus 'facts' are not bases of 'ought'. Whatever may be merit of critiques like G.E. Moore (*Principia Ethica*, 1903) in analysing this truth, we must be careful about levelling any charge of illogic in the name of the "naturalistic fallacy" if there is no *strict* logical derivation, i.e., of the *formal* nature because bereft of any formal derivation, no formal logical fallacy should be levelled, which is another common sense logic, which Moore was reminded of by W.K. Frankena in his seminal essay on "The Naturalistic Fallacy" which proved quite a stuff to defend many touted naturalists like J.S. Mill (*Utilitarianism*, 1957), who would otherwise not to be seen as committing the naturalistic fallacy for he never intended to be either a definist or a formal logical naturalist. Whatever may be the intricacies in the debate, we find that logic is so close to ethics when it comes to ethical arguments for establishing ethical judgements. This is a truism because a *logical inquiry* into the possibility of a strict logical derivation (inductive in this case), of ethical judgements becomes so vital in ethical discourse. Hence, the closeness of ethic and logic is beyond doubt though they belong to different performative classes.

The last point that has been dealt above brings us to the consideration of *strict deductive logical* justification of ethical judgements. Can deductive arguments justify an ethical judgement? Or, can we derive 'is' from 'ought'? We can, but the point is, logically we should not, but why at all do some people think that we can and we should do such things? *Intuitionism* is, broadly speaking, the thesis of a strict deductive derivation of judgements of facts from value, that is, to derive what is the case from what should be the case. Though it is interesting to notice that ethical intuitionism in essence do not agree that any logical argument is needed in the establishment of the indubitable truth of *basic* ethical judgements of value and evaluation, the indubitable judgements are nevertheless, *logical grounds* of deriving specific moral truths about what is done, is in essence ethical. Hence, an attempt to shun logic of any kind in the ethical parlance is not possible. Only when we come to the logical proving of grounds of ethical derivation, do we speak of transcending logic to enter into what is the weird realm of "intuition" or "intuitive justification". This must then beg as said the thinkers like G.E. Moore, H.A. Richard, W.D. Ross, E.F. Carritt and many others that another *more basic* element to justify the basic ground of ethical derivation, which is the intuitive disposition of humans, which is extremely difficult to assert for its "nature" clarification. What interests us here is that despite all attempts to transcend logic, it would not leave them cheaply because intuition as primitive ground for deduction of ethical basic premises cries loud for its own basic logic. Hence, intuitive justification itself begs logic, and thus, the justifying basic premises should show how and why 'is' may be derived from 'ought' as any geometrical axiomatic scheme. And many of us argue that the available logic to support the primitive intuition and the basic premises are fraught with queer epistemic and metaphysical presuppositions which are weak enough. However, we again feel the need of logical inquiry of ethical argun ents and thus the need of logic in ethics.

Is it possible to say that the ethical arguments justifying ethical judgements is *not* strictly logical in any case, but should be understood either as judgements that are proved to be factually or heuristically true or that these judgements are never justified as true or false bereft of what they *do* in ethical contact, that is, how they *function?* The former issue takes us to what was mentioned before as non-formal logical justification of ethical judgements such as verification and heuristic justifications, which are different but not the same, though they are related. The "scientific modes" of justification is an obvious reaction to both the strict logical justifications and non-cognitivism or functionalism as we now understand it after years of debate about subjectivism, emotivism, attitudinalism, prescriptivism and so on. The reasons are simple, first and foremost is that given the positive scientific models of justification of statements, it should be relied on ethical justification because neither strict logical rules nor intuition can help us in ethical matters such as these. Hence, we are left with a strong option of non-intuitive, non-*a priori*, non-metaphysical and non-functional justification, which is *observational*, much like the physical sciences. That the ethical basic principle of universal pleasure maximization holds good or is true in the *propositional sense* begets natural observations of human desires, actions and their consequences. Hence, the scheme must be true of both Bentham's and J.S. Mill's utilitarianism. Simple natural observations and calculus enable us to justify that the basic ethical truth of "Maximum pleasure for maximum number" should be as true as "water is a compound of hydrogen and oxygen" because there is at least one person on earth who *desires* the desirable "pleasure" for him and others and thus the thing must be taken as universally "desirable". It is exactly at this plane of the most awkward scienticism that logic enters in another form, which we call, "informal" logic or simply, "heuristics" or a heuristic understanding of truths. It amounts to be much like a crafty 'art' of drawing inferences from what *is* available to us at the existential level, which enable *us* to justify or understand through most *informal* arguments that such and such value judgements must be true and not false. The reference to such "heuristics" fills the writings of Mill and his supporters. This is, however, a good way to show why Mill was not so easily to be charged for a logical fallacy whether deductive or inductive because he produced none of them, rather an 'informal' or 'heuristic' way to *argue* why the principle of utility must be true, and why "pleasure" has a value and why pleasure seeking is a virtue. Whatever may be the details, again we shall come back to see that even this way of thinking could not shun logical scrutiny. The critiques of scienticism and heuristics show that though there is a problem of justification *in a logical way* to be equated to justification *through logic*, it is very difficult to show that in a 'logical justification' there is *no logic*, even informal logic or heuristics as well as scienticism has its own logic, the deconstruction of which leads us to revelation of fundamental rules of formal logic and their violation. The extreme form of such criticism is that there is no informal logic or better said, informal logic has its own form. The critique argue that though scientific propositions are observationally true or false, their basic principles are *not*, ethical principles may *not* be equally observationally verified, though the ethical judgemental truth, which are particular and not universalizable or basic principles are *not* observationally justifiable either. Even a number of verification fails to justify a particular truth as universal in ethics, which may be true of scientific generalisations as well. That takes us to the logic that in principle though scientific generalisations are *verifiable* or *falsifiable* (*cf.* Karl Popper), ethical generalisations as *generalisable* truths are *not* verifiable or falsifiable in principle. Hence, when we come to the scientific mode of justification and heuristics, inherent logic enable us to argue ethically that in essence, observation justifies judgements, and when we come to its critique, we find that logic tells us as to why that is not the case. In any case, logical scrutiny of ethical matters becomes evident, and with this, their closeness.

With this we now come to the real sceptical challenge, that is, moral arguments necessarily fails at any instance because they rely heavily on or are *contingent on* moral presuppositions, each of them claiming to be true by virtue of sound, logic because their adversaries were not defeated conclusively by their own logic and thus their presuppositions — "How '*x* is good' can be a well founded moral judgement when 'x is bad' can be equally well founded it is not easy to see".[3] This must then take us to the non-cognitive thesis that after all moral judgements of values and evaluation are *not* propositional in nature, they do not possess a truth-value, nor do they have natural and non-natural properties, which are seen to be true, they are non-propositionally true or false. But even this might take us to logical scrutiny, which we shall take up only after we have considered the scepticism about moral arguments. Do moral arguments fizzle out at every instance? The answer is in the affirmative if arguments in favour of '*x* is good' and '*x* is bad' are essentially not to be reconciled because every argument is equally sound, each of them failing to show that the contesting claim is logically fallacious than just showing why their own positions are logically sound. On the other hand, if moral arguments have to sustain their worth, at every instance each argument should provide evidences when needed in its favour and disposed of all counter evidences, which otherwise favour the opponents. When we come to this absorbing logical contest, we enter into what we have been avoiding thus far with regard to logical discussion in ethics, which we termed "moral reasoning". Hence, the final issue of moral argument takes us to "moral reasons". If sceptics need to shut up, moral reasons should not be bundle of non-sense, each tending to be sound, but none really is.

In fact, much heat has been liberated in the dispute over the nature of moral reasons because many people claim that it is not another type of *strict logical reasoning* following the valid rules of deduction and induction, though such reasons do give us conclusions that are said to be proved, indubitable and thus justified for acceptance. Whereas, others claim that moral reasons does not appear to be anything beyond strict logic. And yet, others think that the touted reasons are clatter and platter as none is good than another or, each is as good as another, the point we are considering right now. Though something has been said about the deductive and inductive forms of arguments, we need to add that moral reasons interplaying in these arguments, (a) presuppose *moral universals* acting as premises as sacrosanct as axioms of geometry, though easily noticed counter evidences that destroy the universality thesis, does not hold good; (b) presuppose that *guards against counter evidences* are available not exactly as in the factual sciences rather different, such as revelation, intuition, universalization and inductive subsumption that is complementary to the process; (c) presuppose that there is a *hierarchy of moral universals*, wherein one principle overwhelms another by virtue of its *moral weight* than logical weight though true only in cases of unique conflicts of morality such as in conflict among duties in real life, when *relevance* of one principle over another is morally weighed; and (d) presuppose basic or *normal human sensitivity* to interpret universals in relation to facts. In the face of such stubborn presuppositions, one feels uncomfortable to go along with these deductive moral reasons, particularly for their tough epistemic and ontological presuppositions. However, we need to see that the logical analysis of the model can only reveal the nature and defects of such moral reasons. Similarly, in an inductive moral reason, we may add to what has been said before that it demands, (a) a *continued identity in the situations* or instances, which becomes crucial to subsume a universal principle; and (b) the subsumption is only *probable* though we assume it would lead us to a generalization. The charges against such moral reasons are that neither is there identity among instances nor is there any reason to assume that scientific or probable induction help a generalisation which is sacrosanct. Still better, we are in the realm of logic, which has its play in ethics.

Clearly, with the breakdown of the strict logical reasons in moral justification, we are in hand *non-logical* (not illogical or anti-logical) reasons that justify moral principles and judgements. Hence, we are indirectly suggesting that any logical reason is as good as another but only that they all fail to make a case for ethical justification. We can mention in this regard the sceptical challenges of Stevenson in *Ethics and Language* (1944) and Hare in *The Language of Morals* (1952). These challenges are of great worth. Without answering them we fail to understand why with the end of strict logical reasoning, the systematic mainstream ethical arguments and ethical justifications do not fizzle out. Hence, sceptics are not 'logical nihilists', who argue in favour of 'role of no logic at all in case of establishing ethical judgements' and thus 'no role of logic in ethics' that amounts to saying that 'ethics is bereft of all logic'. Though the arguments of sceptics appear to be heading just towards such uneasy nihilism, still the "logical spirit" has been saved in the ethical parlance, which finally helps us in knowing why without strict logic, ethics can be still "logical" because "being logically grounded" does not beg "being strictly logically grounded", and our sceptics would be so happy to know that they had their own 'logical ethical thesis'. Stevenson, for instance, thinks that ethical conclusions are proved through *non-deductive inference* because ethical conclusions being in nature *emotive* are contingent on expressions of beliefs and attitudes of speaker that is, these are the *causal* grounds of validation of emotive utterances. This would amount to stiff disagreements about the validity of and thus justification or acceptability of value and evaluative statements and, therefore, moral arguments break down. Yet, one needs to refer to the mention of "inference" and "reasons" by Stevenson when he provides his sceptical arguments. He agrees that there is some "reasons" at least, some "inferences" in the offing when we pass moral statements but they are not strictly logical ones. Does that mean that non-deductive reasons bereft us of all logic in ethics? Not to the least because the possibility of non-deductive reasons are strongly supported by Stevenson, the proper construction of which would reveal either a formal pattern in his argument or an informal one, but there is some logic in what he tries to justify. Moreover, logic enables us to refute what he tries to justify for its illogic in a "causal thesis" he propounds because even if ethical conclusions *functions* in *some contexts* as emotive utterances, they are not effects caused by our beliefs and attitudes or are not causes of like or dislike effects on hearers. Doing or *performing* something with ethical statements (and words) is different from causing something or being caused by something. It is only logic and its fallacies that enable us for a critique of his ethical view. Further, drawing from what has been said just now, the 'breakdown' argument itself breaks down because any real life moral disagreement as active in ethical conclusions are neither proved nor justified to be true or false propositionally. Hence, all contesting ethical arguments about values and evaluation 'functions' in a peculiar ethical context to *do something* and to justify that given same logic, one's argument is strong or weak or true or false. Again, stiff ethical disagreements, which are strictly logically irreconcilable does not break down moral arguments in ethics because Stevenson himself argues that we may persuasively or informally justify that certain things need to be accepted for a simple reasonableness or else one takes the risk of being irrational. No one really contests that informal arguments are possible, but we may contest whether they are persuasive in nature or whether any informal argument is in fact, formal in essence.

Hare is careful in mentioning that though moral conclusions

ensue from an argument mostly seen as formal in nature, but the problem is with the major premise of such argument, which is often a universal major premise taking a stiff moral stance, which contests with similar but contrary moral stances, which are irreconcilable, thus amounting to breakdown of moral arguments. This is much in abeyance with what Stevenson has said, particularly in case of whisking off strict logical form in an ethical argument. The intrinsic value of the major premises are thus merely presupposed in an ethical argument which is the most irrational aspect as it appears, or else every reason to accept them are as good as another one. This must be an argument at least, saving logic in ethics as Hare has saved logic, but he takes it away with another hand. Hare tends to forget a brilliant aspect in Stevenson's thesis that in an ethical universalizable statement or an ethical conclusion that might act as a major premise in an ethical argument, the premises are not human predilections because there may be good enough *descriptive arguments* in favour of why something is called good or bad, or right or wrong. As these major premises cannot be arrogantly supported, the contesting conclusions such as "Democracy is good" and "Democracy is bad" is contingent on or is entailed by the descriptive arguments about "Democracy" about whose value we contest. It may well be that there are *evidences* for us to *logically justify* that "Democracy is good" and not "bad" or that "Autocracy is bad and not good. Hence, only if Hare was reminded of this and the basic truth that ethical conclusions may be evidentially strengthened by facts, and that ethical conclusions being not merely functioning as commands as they have descriptive functions and thus correlative meaning, he would not have gone for the breakdown of ethical arguments. The question, "How can evaluative premises be contingent on or be evidenced by non-evaluative ones?" Can still make a case for the sceptics, but as Foot has argued, and I find a good point there but with a difference that the "evidence" or "entailment", should *not* be taken as "observation of hard facts", as it is never needed when descriptive arguments are given to entail why "Democracy" is "good" or "Masochism" is "bad" or "Suicide is bad" or "*Sati* is bad". Such arguments overwhelms in real life situations of moral conflicts where ethical conclusion *appears* to break down but not really so when we consider in confluence of opinions the obvious points to describe a fact that bears a value and not disvalue or the other way round. In reality, hard nuts and headstrongs are outwitted for their arrogance in moral matter based on such simple descriptive arguments. Hence, moral arguments do *not* break down, it enjoys the status in ethics, quite well as logic enjoys the same in ethics.

REFERENCES

1. Ladd, John, *The Structure of Moral Discourse*, Harvard University Press, Harvard, 1957, p.146.
2. Foot, Philippa, "Moral Argument" in Wallace, G. and Walker, A. D. M. (eds.), *The Definition of Morality*, Methuen & Co. Ltd., London, 1970, p. 174.
3. *Ibid.*, p. 174.

Chapter – 6

Role of Argument in Metaethical Theories

Pratima Ganguli

Ethical studies in the west for sometime now have been conducted mainly in a form which is more properly given the name 'Meta-ethics'. In this form ethics has been more a study of Moral terms, concepts, sentences and argument less a study of the factual problems relating to morality such as what action are right and wrong, what things are good and bad, what is our highest good, etc. An idea of what ethical philosophers have been doing in the west for a considerable time now may be had from the following statement of P.H. Nowell-Smith "The task of moral philosopher is to map the mutual relationships of moral words, sentences and arguments. . . ." We shall be concerned here only with the mapping of arguments (in morals) as done by certain eminent moral philosophers of the present time, such as, Stevenson, Toulmin, Hare and N. Smith.

Discussions about argument in morals mainly centre round the following questions: (i) Have arguments any role to play in the sphere of morals? (ii) If so, what is the nature of arguments employed in the sphere of morals? Are they deductive and Inductive? Or if some other specific nature peculiar to morals? (iii) How are the questions of Validity and Invalidity decided with regard to moral arguments?

We shall try to make a comparative and critical evaluation of the views of above four thinkers on each of these three questions. That there is an ample scope for such a study with reference to the above thinkers and that such a study is bound to be interesting and useful from both the logical and moral standpoint, may be seen to some extent into the following brief account of the views of each of the above thinkers.

Moore, from whom recent ethics takes its start distinguishes between two sorts of questions that should be asked in any proper ethical enquiry (i) What kind of things are intrinsically good; and (ii) What actions ought we to perform? He points out no proof or argument could be given to show that certain things were good. That something is good could be seen only intuitively. However, proof in a causal sense could be given with regard to the answer to the second question. But again such proof never takes the form of a logical argument. Moore, therefore, on the whole, remain an intuitionist and at least in his *Principia Ethica* does not seem to give much value to arguments in Ethics. Prichard in his famous article "Does moral philosophy rest on a mistake", severely criticises any attempt to base any theory of obligation in arguments.

It is Stevenson who at least apparently seems to recognize the value of presenting arguments or giving reasons in matters of morals. Of course, it is yet to be seen, whether, what Stevenson takes as moral arguments can really be called so in any logical sense or not. But then it is a fact that he talks of giving reason in ethics and also discusses at length the question of validity and invalidity of what he calls moral arguments. For Stevenson, occasion for argument in moral arises when two people disagree regarding a moral issue. Such disagreements are of two types according to him — Disagreement in belief and disagreement in attitude. Disagreement in belief is resolvable by citing empirical evidence. It needs "detailed sensitive attention" as Stevenson himself writes that no problems peculiar to moral reasoning arise in connection with it. If we disagree, for example, regarding the belief of the exact date of our last meeting we can very well verify the case both inductively and deductively. We can ask about it from several persons who were present there at our meeting spot or, we may turn over the pages of our personal diary where we generally use to write all the important incidents of our lives. Stevenson believes that this type of argument which can very well be used in course of moral reasoning is perfectly helpful in dissolving moral disagreements in belief.

But the case is not so easy with disagreement in attitude. It cannot be resolved only by citing empirical evidences. Disagreement in attitude continues even if disagreement in belief dissolves.

Stevenson has invented a new device which he has termed as "persuasive method" to dissolve the disagreement in attitude which is not simply concerned with facts. This, according to him is the second type of argument in moral discourse. As the very relation between belief and attitude according to Stevenson is psychological, so he believes that disagreement in attitude can be resolved by persuasive method only, which works through emotional appeal and imperative suggestion and thus helps to redirect the attitude of the person concerned.

Stevenson maintains that persuasive methods are non-rational (not irrational) in the sense that they are not based upon factual or logical reasons, rather are concerned mainly with our feelings or emotion. The power of effectiveness of this method chiefly depends upon the impact of ethical predicates having emotive meaning. As Stevenson writes "the most important of the non-rational methods, the persuasive in a somewhat broader sense, depends on direct emotional impact of words on emotive meaning, rhetorical cadence, apt metaphor, Stentorian, stimulating or pleading tone of voice, dramatic gestures, care in establishing rapport with the hearer or audience and so on".

Stevenson strongly criticises those who condemn persuasive method as bad and wish to adopt only rational methods to end moral disputes. He further says that persuasive methods are not only used to redirect other's attitude but often used to make private decision regarding what is good or bad, right or wrong.

Finally, there is a third type of argument which Stevenson calls 'Giving Reasons'. Sometimes disagreement in question involves both attitudes and beliefs. One has to produce an argument designed to change both the beliefs and attitude of the opponent. Giving reasons according to Stevenson bringing forth such statement of belief and attitude before the moral disputant so as to bring him to the level of agreement. This can be best understood in the light of Stevenson's own model of analysing ethical judgement, such as '*X* is good'.

According to Stevenson what someone really means by the above judgement may be analysed in the following form:

I approve of X;
Do so as well.

Reasons to proof the first statement can be given by bringing in factual evidences in support of speaker's approval of *X*. Similarly, reasons for the imperative or the second sentence can also be given though not strictly in scientific sense but in another sense typical to commands or imperatives. If for example anyone issues a command 'close the door' and the hearer asks 'why', then the person issuing command may give reason 'because cold wind is blowing'. It is not irrelevant in case of moral arguments.

Now, the question arises as to how we evaluate the soundness of argument of these three types? In other words, how do we distinguish the valid from the invalid arguments in each of these three groups? The questions of validity is easily answered, Stevenson claims with respect to the first two. With respect to the third type of argument, however, the question is rather complicated. Here, although we do not speak of deduction or induction, but we do speak of inference. We make a transition from a factual reason to ethical conclusion. As Stevenson himself says "One of the peculiarities of ethical arguments lies in the inference from a factual reason to an ethical conclusion". The question, therefore, arises— "Is there some other kind of validity, peculiar to normative arguments"? After some reflexion Stevenson decides to answer the question in the negative. He says that the term 'valid' is intimately connected with the term 'true'. But because ethical judgements can neither be called true nor false in any real sense of the terms, therefore, ethical arguments can neither be called valid nor invalid in any 'helpful-sense' of the terms. Its validity or invalidity in its typical sense means its acceptance or rejection.

Toulmin in his attempt to base morality on reason in the logical sense of the term criticises both Moore and Stevenson, the first for his failure to recognize reason as the proper guide of morality and instead taking intuition to be the real guide and the second for his treatment of moral arguments in such a manner that they could be neither valid nor invalid in any proper logical sense. As to the primacy of the place of reason in ethics, Toulmin declares that we should not follow in the footsteps of Moore in taking the analysis of the term 'good' to be the primary business of Ethics. The very first question that we should read in ethics should rather be the following— "What reasons are good reasons for an ethical conclusions"?

Against Stevenson Toulmin points out that with regard to moral arguments questions of validity and invalidity are not irrelevant. There is a sense in which moral arguments are valid and invalid. Moral reasoning is called by Toulmin 'Evaluative inference', which according to him is an inference from factual premises to an ethical conclusion. Curiously enough, Stevenson had also said the same thing, with regard to moral inferences, but, whereas he hardly saw any logical points involved in such inferences, the former finds such inferences involving important logical points. Of course, Toulmin admits that in the perfectly normal sense of the terms, moral arguments can either be called deductive, or inductive. They are in a sense peculiar to Ethics. Still, the questions of validity and invalidity may be meaningfully raised and answered in the case of these arguments. Toulmin agrees with Stevenson that the questions of validity and invalidity are intimately connected with questions of truth and falsity of the judgement. He, however, disagrees with Stevenson in so far as the latter holds that ethical judgements could not be held true-false. The following two ideas basically separate Toulmin from both Moore and Stevenson:

(i) That moral judgements, although they do not refer to anything, are capable of being called true and false and contradictory to each other.

(ii) That we can properly and legitimately speak of moral arguments from factual premise to ethical conclusions and correspondingly, we can also speak of validity and invalidity of these arguments.

According to Toulmin, questions of truth and validity are not two separate questions in moral discourse. He invokes his theory of 'good-reasons' to point out that to say a moral judgement to be true is to say nothing else than, that, there are good reasons to support it And this amounts to the same thing as saying that here is a valid inference from certain factual premises to the moral judgement. Now the question arises what reasons are worthy of acceptance? Toulmin answers that there are two kinds of good moral reasoning:

(i) Reasoning concerned with justifying a particular action showing the chosen action to be a dugy, i.e. to be demanded by the moral code of one's community.

(ii) Reasoning which is concerned with the justification of a practice by reference to the ideal. Such a justification, in short, shows that the practice in question is conducive to the well-being or happiness of others in the community.

Toulmin calls the first one "Argument from duty" and the second one as "Arguments from the welfare of our fellows".

On the basis of the above, Toulmin's moral arguments may be put in the following form:

(a) *P* is *R* (where *R* is a moral code of the community) P is right

(b) *S* is conducive to social harmony *S* is right.

Although at the first glance both the above arguments seem to have opposite faces, but closer observation will reveal the fact that both can be expressed in the same form as follows:

(a) Whatever is accepted in the moral code is right, *P* is accepted in the moral code
P is right.

(b) Whatever is conducive to social harmony is right, *S* is conducive to social harmony
S is right.

Hence, it is clear that the factor which guarantees our passage from the factual premises to the ethical conclusion, according to Toulmin is based on some sort of rule of inference which he calls 'The principle of social harmony'.

As it has already been discussed that Toulmin bothers little regarding the logical validity and invalidity of moral arguments. He clearly says that moral judgements are true or false, and, accordingly moral arguments are valid or invalid. Toulmin believes that in ethics we are faced with a special sort of reasoning which is different from that employed in formal logic or in empirical science.

Hare in his prescriptivism has no doubt regarding the role of arguments in morals. The function of moral judgements according to him is to guide our conduct, rather to persuade someone as Stevenson believes it to be. Hare himself says, "The language of morals is sort of prescriptive language". The nature of prescriptive language is such that it entails imperatives or commands. To prescribe is to issue commands, and to issue commands is to speak the language of imperatives. Both moral judgements and imperative have similarities as well as differences, which Hare has termed as 'Phrastic' and 'Neustic'. Phrastic marks the common bond between them, but neustic marks their difference while following the foot-steps of Kant, Hare believes that moral judgements are universal in nature, whereas, imperatives are not necessarily so. Thus, prescriptivity and universalisability are two essential characters of moral judgements according to Hare.

Throughout his ethical writings specially in his second book *Freedom and Reason*. Hare has been anxious to give emphasis that moral judgements must be supported by reasons. He clearly mentions that it is not obligatory for the imperatives to be supported by reason, but moral judgements must always be supported by reasons. He agrees with Toulmin in the point that moral argument can be called valid and invalid, but then he does not agree with him, that, moral arguments are peculiar to ethics and that the questions of their validity and invalidity could be analytically decided as in the case of ordinary deductive arguments. For Hare, moral arguments are perfectly deductive and analytic in nature and the questions of their validity and invalidity are decided in the same manner in which they are decided in the case of ordinary deductive arguments. Hare argues, to a very great length that imperatives follow logical rules just as indicatives and may contradict and entail one another.

Both Stevenson and Toulmin had pointed out that moral arguments consisted in deriving an evaluative conclusion from one or more factual premises. But Hare, as opposed to both declares as a matter of rule that no evaluative conclusion can be validity drawn from a set of premises which does not contain at least one evaluative premise. Hare clearly echoes the famous Humean note that 'ought' cannot be derived out of 'is', that from purely factual premises no ethical conclusion can be drawn. To look all these points in their greater details, will be very prolonged study which we cannot accomplish here, in this short article.

Hare's interest in moral arguments, however, is not confined only to seeing how a moral conclusion can be validly derived out of premises, one of which is a universal evaluative and the other a factual one. His interest is extended through the logic of moral arguments in the above sense to the general logic of imperatives. Here the main point to be considered is that whenever some moral advice is given to someone in the form of an imperative or a command, in what will lie the carrying of the command or the imperative. In other words, whenever a command is given what are the further command or imperatives that are implied by the original command. Hare also argues that the pattern of implication or entailment in the case of imperatives is the same as it is in the case of indicatives. On the whole he argues that the logic of imperatives is essentially the same as the logic of indicatives. We can illustrate his views in this regard by means of an example. In the ordinary logic of indicatives the argument of the from *P* and *Q*, *P* is deemed to be a perfectly valid argument. Can, on this basis it be said that in the sphere of imperatives also we can make a valid argument of a similar form? Can we for example, from the premise 'Put on your Parachute and jump out' draw the conclusion 'jump out'? If yes, then doing of the latter will be regarded as doing the former itself. But apparently it looks odd. Carrying out the command 'jump out' is not the same as 'Put on your Parachute and jump out'. How can it be said then that the pattern of inference in the case of imperatives is the same as it is in the case of indicatives? Hare argues that there is nothing wrong on the logical level in drawing out the above kind of inference. This will be clear if we try to understand things by distinguishing between necessary conditions and sufficient conditions of the justification of belief of proposition. In all deductive inference believing in the truth of the conclusion is a necessary condition of believing in the truth of premises. But it is never a sufficient condition also. Similar is the case with the above imperative inference also. Fulfilling the command 'jump out' is a necessary condition of the fulfilment of the command 'Put on your Parachute' and 'jump out' but it is not a sufficient condition. So in deriving jump out from 'Put on your Parachute and jump out' one does not make any mistake in point of logic. His inference is of the same nature as that of any ordinary deductive inference. The error lies, therefore, not in making any invalid inference, but in fulfilling a command which is not a sufficient condition for fulfilment of the original command. In Hare's words the error consists "not in making an invalid inference but in fulfilling the weaker command when what I gave him was the stronger".

As it sees quite natural from the above, Hare's notion of the validity and invalidity of moral arguments is exactly the same as these notions are employed in ordinary deductive logic. N. Smith seems to hold that moral arguments are not strictly deductive and analytic in nature as Hare holds them to be. Consequently, the question of their validity and invalidity also cannot be decided in the same manner as they did in case of deductive argument. N. Smith seems to substitute in moral context the notion of contextual implication for logical implication or entailment. And the notion of 'logical Oddness' for self contradiction or invalidity. According to him factual premises may constitute reason for a moral conclusion but the latter is not entailed by the former. It is simply contextually implied by the former, such that to hold the premises and deny the conclusion will not be self contradictory but only logically odd. N. Smith defines the context of contextual implication and logical oddness in perfectly precise terms and views the moral arguments with reference to these context as well as with reference to his concept of the Pro and Con words and attitude. As a matter of fact, N. Smith does not find worthwhile for a moral philosopher to see in moral context, what statement entails what and what statements contradicts what. The task of a moral philosopher in his own words is "Not of showing how one statement entails or contradicts another but of showing that in a certain context it would be logically odd to assert one thing and deny another." All these points really deserve detail analysis.

On the basis of the above we must have a brief idea as to how all the philosophers mentioned and make very valuable and interesting contributions regarding the role and the nature of arguments in morals as well as regarding the questions of validity and invalidity of such arguments.

REFERENCES

A.J. Ayer, *Language, Truth and Logic*.

C.L. Stevenson, *Ethics and Language*, Yale University Press, 1966, Facts and Value.

Freedom and Reason, Oxford University Press, 1963.

G.C. Kerner, *The Revolution in Ethical Theory*, Oxford University Press.

G.E Moore , *Principia Ethics*, Cambridge University Press, 1960.

H.A. Prichard, Does Moral Philosophy on a Mistake, *Mind*, Vol. XXI, 1912.

J.O. Urmson, The Emotive *Theory of Ethics*, Hutchinson Library, 1968. 1966.

P.H. Nowell Smith, *Ethics*, Penguin Books Ltd., 1954.

R.C. Cross, Ethical Disagreement, *Philosophy*, Vol. 25, 1950.

R.M. Hare, *Language of Morals*, Oxford University Press, 1952.

W.D. Ross, *Foundations of Ethics*, Oxford: The Clarendon Press, 1939.

Chapter – 7

Moral Reasoning

Veena Kapoor

We often argue for or against the value judgements, the moral principles or statements that we make. Problems of ethics are evidently not concerned with personal feelings, or the outcome of subjective relations and personal impressions. They cannot be explained away just by saying what is attractive or desirable to a particular individual. To judge actual or possible actions as right or wrong, good or bad is not only to know psychological and physiological conditions of a person but it is about the rightness and goodness of the action. We cannot base our moral judgements on phantasies and whims, for we must have some rational grounds for approving of some actions and disapproving of others. If we evaluate that some past deed was 'good' or some proposed course of action is 'right', it is certainly not enough for us to know the way we are disposed to evaluate the action; or say that it seems to me the best way of judging or doing the action. For, such a judgement requires reasons for the action which we think as worthy of approval.

The whole problem arises regarding what sort of reasons could be taken as worthy of approval, or so to say good reasons. The phrase 'good reason' is ambiguous which may mean the factual explanations which could be given for some action and as such exempting the agent from any moral responsibility. We may justify the validity of actions by referring to certain principles, strictly speaking, not chosen by ourselves, but just being committed to them by being a member of a particular society. Such principles in themselves may not be called moral but mere social norms, however, the very commitment of a person to these principles by being the citizens of that state, is moral in nature. For example, Socrates sacrificed his life on the grounds that once we accept to be in a particular state, under the dominion of the laws of the state, we cannot escape our duty of abiding by these norms. On the other hand, good reasons logically may mean to argue about the validity or the invalidity of the argument which again will leave no room for further questioning to *"what shall we do"* or " why did we do the way we did?" In so far these types of reasoning will be of little help in grasping ethical problems, we will have to find the solution for the problem somewhere else. After all, what is the nature of ethical reasoning? What kind of argument, or reasoning is proper for us to accept in support of mora ldecisions? Neither empirical laws of human behaviour nor mere logical reasoning are sufficient to make us understand the nature of moral reasoning. Toulmin very rightly contends that "Reasons being offered in support of conclusions are so many and so diverse that it is hard to see what is common to them and the choice is embarrassing".[1] Through examples, he shows that how reasons are diverse in different fields. The only common element among all these sorts of reasoning is that of dialectic.

There is no doubt and dispute regarding the moral problems and their solutions that they take place in concrete social circumstances. Here circumstances include the social condition psychological state of mind of individual and physiological basis of man. It may be argued that we cannot talk of good or bad irrespective of that to which they refer., i.e., to say that we can talk of good conduct, good action, good object or good relationships. The meaning of morality becomes worthwhile only in the living context. But the question arises whether social context could be taken as the neccessary and sufficient factor determining conditions of morality is empirical reference sufficient for understanding and justifying morality? And whether there is moral basis of social organization or social basis of moral conduct. It seems, it will not be inappropriate to maintain that there holds a dynamic relationship between the two. Each supporting the other in practical matters.

The question regarding reasoning arises either when person is puzzled about the course of action he should take up as best: or when two or more than two principles conflict with each other claiming to be equally worthwhile and the decider or adviser has to find out principle to act upon. It may also be argued that the best course of action would be that which is consistent and is in accordance with certain rules. In so far as we are concerned with the derivation of conclusion from the given rules, the moral reasoning may be analogous to that of logical reasoning, that is, from the given premises, the conclusion is made explicit. However, ethical reasoning is not strictly formal in nature. Its enquiry does not stop here because we need to explore the nature of principles themselves which cannot be established merely by basing them on logical reasoning. We are concerned with practical and specific issues which take place in new situations forcing us to reformulate the given principles in the light of those situations forcing us to reformulate the given principles in the light of those situations. The argument in ethical discourse as such remains no more formal and logical but requires knowledge of circumstances as well. Aristotle long ago emphasized the nature of practical syllogism in the context of incontinence. Accordingly, the major premise is an opinion which makes a general statement about the class of particular things and the minor premise is the particular instance of the class of things and the minor premise is the particular instance of the class of things. He says, "when the two premises are combined to form the syllogism, we have a result analogous to what we have in the pure ratiocination. As in the latter, the mind is forced to affirm the conclusion so in the practical syllogism we are forced straightaway to do it. Suppose, you have these premises. "All sweet things ought to be tasted" and "that thing is sweet",[2] when these premises are brought into relation you are bound, if nothing prevents you and you can do it, to go and taste the thing."[3]

To the question how did one arrive at a particular moral

judgement, the answer is to be sought in the principle in which the judgement itself is implicit and may be made explicit in the conclusion. So the problem is not much, as to how to make a moral judgement but how to decide for moral principles deciding for moral principles would be different from making moral judgements which perhaps may be the derivation of conclusions from the given principles. As Aristotle says: "Now there may be simultaneously present in the mind two universal judgements, one saying you must not taste", the other, "every sweet thing is pleasant." When this happens, and then the minor premise "That thing is sweet" presents itself, while at the same time desire is present, then in spite of the fact that the first universal bids you avoid the thing in question, the desire leads you to it. It is, therefore, we conclude, to some extent an intellectual principle or opinion which influences the incontinent man to behave as he does, an opinion not in itself contradictory of the right principle but only opposed to it by an accidental conjunction of circumstances. This is the reason why the lower animals are not incontinent. They are incapable of understanding a generalization: all they have is mental images and the memory of particular objects.

After all, what kind of reasons are those which guide and prescribe us to do something. Under the cover of cognitivism it may be stated that either they are likely to produce the best results or that they are the instances of a rule of action giving rise to modern doctrines of moral standards, so called (i) result or telelogical ethical theories; and (ii) formal or deontological ethical theories. Cognitive ethical theories establish a type of empirical or scientific or intuitive reasoning by means of which moral or practical questions may be answered. For teleologists or naturalists, moral words are definable in non-moral principles is possible in the same manner as in factual ones. For example, R.B. Perry says that good is an object of interest, and right is conducive to harmonious happiness. Or as for Hume, good or bad is entirely based upon factual and theoretical considerations about human nature and society. Or for J.S. Mill, what is most desirable is good and what is most desirable is desired by most of the people.

For deontologists the principle ought to be respected for its own sake. For instance we refer to intuition, or God given principles, or Kantian Moral Law as reasons for justifying rightness and wrongness of the action. Such principles are self-evident and true in themselves, therefore, are absolute. Socrates and Kant gave highest priority to Moral Law. It is the reverence for law which makes a person reason in accordance with the principle. Socrates took hemlock for the sake of duty. For Socrates and Kant promise ought to be kept for its own sake. On the other hand according to result theorists, we should keep promise because not doing so will lead to suffering and we should try to avoid such undesirable results. We give reasons while making decisions regarding principles which regulate and control our conduct and guide us the way we ought to behave to attain some end.

It may also be argued that the whole problem regarding ethical reasoning may arise because of the ambiguity involved in the very use of the value terms like: ought, good or right. These terms have non-moral and moral use as well. For example, its non-moral use "What one ought to do to analyse the water components"? And it is not difficult to show by making an experiment that water is the resultant of H_2O. Whereas, in its moral use a person has to decide for a principle in certain situations when confronted with such a problem "What ought I do to be good". And this practical issue cannot be dealt with that ease because of its open endedness. An action can be performed in several alternate ways and any factual information can merely report to us what is the case and not what ought to be the case.

So wrote David Hume more than two hundred years ago. The question as posed in the following argument is as alive today as it was then. That is how do we get ethical conclusion from non-ethical premises? "He will cause her a great deal of suffering if he leaves her", is a statement of empirical fact (which may be true or false), but how do we get from this the ethical conclusion. "Therefore he ought not to leave her?"[4] Hume says understanding morality involves understanding why and how such a thing happens at all. Why do we have particular attitudes towards actions and why do we approve or disapprove of them? For Hume, feeling plays an important role in making moral judgements. What a person actually feels determines his moral judgement. Hence, without appropriate feeling there would be no such thing as moral judgement. So, he says, morality is not a matter of reason but of feeling. Reason alone can never be the motive to any action of the will and secondly it can never oppose passion in the direction of the will. Reason cannot prevent volition, is incapable of disputing the preference with any passion or emotion. Reason is and ought to be the slave of passion. It is because of the special character of moral judgements that they cannot be perceived by reason. There are feelings of approbation and disapprobation and the moral judgement is the result of the expression of those feelings. In certain cases, we express feeling by way of making an assertion. They are not just like ejaculations, cries or cheer as has been held by logical positivists. (A.J. Ayer, R. Carnap, Richards and Richards). "Once we come to have certain beliefs about the way things are, then, because of natural human dispositions we feel certain sentiments which we express in moral judgements.

Because of the significance that Hume gave to feeling in morality, he is sometimes misconstrued as non-cognivist. He does not reject the knowability of these feeling of approbation and disapprobation of which the moral judgement is the outcome. Because he completely rejects the possibility of rational justification, it does not mean that ethical judgements are mere hues and cries, rather, as he says, they are the sentiments expressed through moral judgements and these sentiments could be explained most appropriately in terms of natural human dispositions.

The problem is that whether cognitivists are doing anything more than mere reporting facts, i.e. to say that there is a feeling, interest or desire for happiness which could be cognised. But how to derive an 'ought-statement' from ' is-statement'? After all what is the nature of inference that an ethical naturalist makes from the facts and psychological theories to ethical principle? Whether it is inductive or deductive or it has peculiar nature of its own. Logically speaking, no deduction of ought-statement is possible from 'is-statement'. This leads us to another doctrine which holds that ethical principles are analytic and self-evident in character and may be known to us through intuition. Moral reasoning, for the intuitionists, rests upon a direct awareness of duty, and obligation gives the word 'right' its meaning, e.g. G.E. Moorean intuitionist, accuses all the naturalists for committing naturalistic fallacy. Naturalistic fallacy is the typical error for using it. Non-cognitivists disagree with him that ethical terms could be ascribed any property at all. For Moore, Good has a non-natural property which can be a matter of knowledge and as such known to us through intuition. For non-cognitivists ethical reasoning is best understood in point of meaning and function of ethical utterances. Stevenson assigns emotive meaning to ethical utterances in addition to descriptive meaning.[5] The descriptive meanings of the words do not tell us anything more than what do they actually represent whereas, it is the emotive meaning which casually influences and persuades people to act in a certain manner. Emotive meaning has the dynamic purpose of evoking an attitude of commendation or contempt in the hearer. As such, why an action should be or should not be performed, will ultimately depend on the emotive use of the ethical language. Emotive meaning is a tendency of the word-arising through the history of its usage, to produce (result from) affective responses in people.[6] R.M. Hare, on the other hand, suggests that the special sort of meaning is not the emotive meaning but prescriptive meaning which is not to be taken as a mode of casually influencing the attitudes, but what we may call an imperative guiding or prescribing.

Hare in his book *The Language of Morals* confines to the point of view that ethical language has logical properties from which emerges a theory of moral reasoning. He develops a morally neutral theory of moral reasoning, however, having moral, relevance. In his book: *Freedom and Reason* he concedes to what Popper says: "There is no reasoning which proceeds from the data of observation to the truth of a hypothesis. Scientific inquiry is rather a kind of exploration, or looking for hypothesis which will stand up to the test of experiment........Moral reasoning......... too is a kind of exploration and not a kind of linear inferences, and that the only inferences which take place in it are deductive".[7]

He also believes that underlying these neutral logical properties of moral language, there is a substantive moral view, i.e. utilitarian view. The basic features of moral language that underlie Hare's theory are prescriptivity of moral judgements and the universalizeability of moral reasons. Taken together these distinct features of moral arguments require that the reasons cited by one person to justify an action will be taken as morally good reasons in the case of any other person. The universalizability, Hare contends, lies in the very use of the moral term 'ought'. For example "No one ever is to smoke in this compartment" is a statement which amounts to saying that in time to now no one is to smoke in a particular compartment and is equally prescriptive to everyone, that is, whosoever, if happens to be in the similar type of compartment, ought not to smoke.

Moral argument is universalizable not only in one sense but in double sense. First, it is universalizable for the person concerned only, that if he himself happens to be in similar situations again, he will act accordingly; secondly, if any one else also happens to be in the similar situation and has similar reasons to perform the action his action to that extent is justified. The contention here made by Hare does not make the principle analytic or *a priori* one. Because of the element of prescriptivity everyone is free to make decision for himself keeping in view that it will be contradictory to say that I ought to do it but you ought not, even if circumstances is the same in both the cases. Any universalizable-prescriptive principle tells others to make the case and not to get it done. The universalizability of principle lies in a particular context and in so far as context differs from person to person we can think of many specific but universalizable principles. As such there cannot be one single ultimate, self-evident, analytic or *a priori* principle to apply to justify actions.

The universalizability of moral principles and judgements as reason may have a direct relation with the pro-attitude of the speaker and hearer as well, says Nowell-Smith. It would be absurd to say "This is good, but I don't advice you do do it" or as to say that "This is the best course, but shall I take it? The good reasons that apply to good in the context of choice apply equally in the context of advice with one difference only, that is (because of the fact) that the problem to be solved is now someone else's with same contextual implications. To tell someone that something is the best course of action is to advice him to do it, but irresponsibly. For the good reasons involved in advising would be the same if the advisor would have to make a choice for himself. It is assumed that the speaker knows the problem and his advice is relevant in accordance with the relevant pro-attitude of the hearer. The basis of making a choice the way we make is the pro and con-attitudes". Pro-words differ from each other in many ways but they all have this in common: that they provide logically impossible explanations of why someone chose to do something.[8] Further Nowell Smith says: "To the questioning of criteria there is no end, but if we ask whether the criteria for judging are good criteria we must, at whatever level we have reached, use criteria for deciding whether these are good or not ...... The self-guaranteeing criteria so vainly sought by some moralist are neither possible nor necessary."[9]

Persuasively argued by many writers such as Philllippa Foot, Toulmin, Searle. G.J.Warock, Anscombe, Kurt Baier, etc., that being in a particular society one cannot think of criteria of moral value other than the descriptive term learned in the cultural group suggesting a specific form of moral life (as such making a reference to institutional fact which differ from brute facts). For this kind of argument may help us in supporting our argument but cannot give us a sound justificative argument to explain the validity of ultimate principles nor can the problem of the logical link between the descriptive criteria and moral evaluation be explained. For instance Toulmin argues "that ethical arguments, are arguments designed to influence behaviour seems hardly worth mentioning, the real problem, which ..... remain as unanswered as ever, is not whether, but in what respect we are to let them influence our behaviour" and " to which arguments (ethical, needless to say) are we to pay attention, and which are we to reject, when making up our minds what to do?

He further says: "Ethics is concerned with the harmonious satisfaction of desires and interest. On most occasions it is a good reason for choosing or approving of an action that it is in accordance with an established maxim of conduct, forth existing moral code, and the current institutions and laws, provide the most reliable guide as to which decisions will be happy in the same kind of way as codes of standard practice in engineering." Such a good reasoning approach which refers to institutional facts looks like a substantive moral principle in disguise. Thus once again we are pushed back to the position taken by non-cognitivists (Hare, Stevenson, Nowell-Smith, and Bernard Mayo) that each person must finally choose his own principles or moral criteria. Whether it is an emotivists or a prescriptivist or an intuitionist takes ultimately refuge in the self decided moral principles. For Max, Nowell Smith and Mayo, etc., consistency and universalizability are the criteria of ethical judgements. From a purely logical point of view any principle can be a moral principle, and any fact can be a good moral reason for any judgement or any decision. You simply choose whatever principle will provide the appropriate syllogistic connction.

The problem underlies the argument as developed by Harian traditions is that, can morally good reasons fully be explained in terms of logically good reasons? Can we justify the nature of moral principles by clarifying the meanings of terms employed in ethical language? It is suggested that universalizability is the primary feature of a moral argument, i.e., to say that if a moral principle is defied or changed frequently from time to time then it cannot be taken as a moral principle. But it is not true with all sort of principles, moral or no-moral? For consistency is the condition to be fulfilled by any of the action in order to be called an action. All sorts of happenings cannot be called actions, and universalizability tends to give reasons for actions. Therefore, universalizability is simply that which value-judgements share with descriptive judgements. In *Freedom and Reason*, Hare mentions that moral arguments own their cogency to a combination of factors: (1) facts,

(2) logic (prescriptivity and universalizability), (3) inclination and interest, and (4) power of imagination and impartial judgement. It is argued that no argument, however, starts from nothing. We must therefore, ask what are the basic requirement of moral arguments. The first essential ingredient of moral argument is that the facts of the case should be given and defined; prescriptivity and universalizability being its logical factors cannot be denied and looking to the interests of making an impartial view. Giving weight to other's interests turns the selfish prudential reasoning into moral reasoning, says Hare.

As such we find, whether it is an emotivist or prescriptivist, or attitudinist all lay emphasis ultimately on the point that it is not at all possible for us to make moral decisions unless and until we refer to interests and facts (for Hare) or pro-attitudes (for Nowell-Smith and Stevenson). Will not the very introduction of these terms reduce their accountability somehow to interest theory or attitudinist theory? How to reconcile the logical argument and interest theory endorsed for ethical reasoning? And can we be fully aware of other's interest attitudes or inclinations? Also, the problem is regarding the formulation of these attitudes. Are they natural or acquired? This will give rise to a further problem, whether it is the pro-or con-attitudes or interests themselves be taken as good reasons or we can look for still other good reasons for formulating pro-, or con-attitudes. How can we universalize an interest or a pro- and con-attitude? It may be said that when a person starts looking into the matter disinterestedly, impartially and sincerely that he can understand "What is good". It is the reflective to good reasons possible by transcending one's jealousy and hatred. It is not that reason should not be listened to, for it would be rather a tautologous question "Should I follow a reason" like "is a circle a circle" or "why should I follow a reason", like ("Why is a circle a circle"). Impartiality and sincerity are the basic factors to the problem and not only the emotions of individual.

Since man is the combination of his rational and irrational constituents, the decision regarding moral principle is not an easy task. This complicated task can be looked into by reflecting on the situations thoroughly. It seems that universalizability criterion and principle of consistency are the essential ingredients of moral argument but they alone we cannot be able to say with certainty, "but why it is moral?" Therefore, we may say that problem of ethical reasoning may be studied by giving due weight to the motives, deliberative and reflective desires, intentions, in terest on the one hand, and to the effects (actual or possible) on the other, as is required on the occasion. It seems that one have to put oneself in the place of others to have a sincere and impartial vision of the matter which is not possible only by reflective thinking but by devotion also. If personal liking overcomes while making moral judgements, principles or statements. All these factors taken together may give us an understanding of ethical reasoning.

REFERENCES

1. S. Toulmin, *An Examination of the Place of Reason in Ethics.* Cambridge. The University Press, 1961, pp. 68-69.
2. Aristotle, *Nicomachean Ethics,* Tr. by J.A.K. Thomson, Penguin Books, 1963, pp. 200-201.
3. D. Hume, *Enquiries concerning the Human Understanding and Concerning the Principle of Moral,* Ed. By L.A.Selby-Bigge, Oxford.The Clarendon Press, 1951, p. 419.
4. *Ibid.,* pp. 468-469.
5. C.L. Stevenson, *Ethics and Language*, New Haven, London, Yale University Press, 1944, p.33.
6. R.M. Hare. *Freedom and Reason*, London, the Clarendon Press, 1963, p. 88.
7. PH. Nowell-Smith, *Ethics*, Penguin Books Ltd., England, 1969, p.114.
8. *Ibid.*, p.175.
9. S.Toulmin, *op. cit.,* 130.
10. *Ibid.*, p. 233.
11. R.M. Hare, *Freedom and Reason,* pp. 93-94.

Chapter – 8

Means and Ends

R.S. Bhatnagar

If there is an end or objective to be achieved there must be a means to achieve it and if one wants to achieve something, one has to adopt appropriate means to achieve it and there ends the business. Why should then there be a problem regarding the relationship between means and ends or the problem regarding the propriety of means?

Normally, if one wants to acquire knowledge or some skill, one is supposed to go to an institution or to some expert or *guru*; if one wants a job one has to acquire appropriate skills or expertise and then apply for the job; if one wants to run a business one has to invest money and apply the rules of the trade; and if one wants to win an election, one has to prove that one is the only suitable candidate and has to canvas for it. So where is the problem?

I can see the philosopher smiling mildly on my naivety. If the matter were really so simple why should there have been a debate about the fairness or goodness of means? What does it mean to say that apart from the ends, means should also be good. Once the Pandora's box is opened there arise several questions to be answered.

As is well known the question relating to means got into focus in the context of Gandhian movement. There were alternative ways of social change available. French Revolution and Russian

Revolution led to drastic social and political changes and it was said that these revolutions involved violent strategies. In contrast, Gandhi proposed a non-violent technique to revolutionise the society and the polity: *Satyagraha* was one fundamental method adopted and was brought into practice as a method of social change.

It is a fact of history that we had to wage a long struggle in order to win freedom from the foreign rule. If all the movements directed towards one single aim of achieving freedom from the foreign yoke are taken into account a wide spectrum of strategies can be described· Attempts made in 1857 were obviously violent confrontations with the British, later again there were people who did not believe in the soft approach and wanted to confront the foreign rulers with strong might. There were moderates who thought that peaceful negotiations would win them their goal. There were *krantikaris* who thought that the only way to turn the British out of the country was violent strategy. There were revolts for rightful rights, such as the naval revolt and, of course, Gandhian *satyagraha* was almost pivotal. Gandhi's suspension or withdrawal from all India *Satyagraha* because of Chaurichaura incident divided the opinion between violent and non-violent approaches.

This short description makes it clear that it is very difficult to ascribe exclusive credit to any one approach as a consequence of which we had Independence. And this phenomenon perpetuates the debate as to what means could be proper in order to attain an objective.

Is there a simple one-to-one relationship between means and ends? Is means something amenable to clear and precise definition. Do means remain means and ends are ends? Does the problem remains same in the context of an individual striving and a corporate movement? The well known Indian wisdom recommending fourfold approaches of *sama*, *dama*, *danda* and *bheda* are meaningless? Or the well known adage highlighted in *Mahabharata* — *Ahimsa* as *paramodharmah* has no wisdom? These questions require a preliminary enquiry into the nature of action for both ends and means form its main constituents.

As soon as you think of action, *Gita*'s statement comes to mind "the nature of *karma* is a profound matter". *Gita*'s *sloka* 18.14 lists the basic constituents of action — locus, agent, means, effort and chance (I am using chance for *daiva*). It would be convenient to concentrate on agent and means and going into their details would mean that we will have to go out of the context of *Gita*.

This does not mean that whatever else is found in *Gita* about action is not relevant. We shall have occasion to refer to those considerations as and when the need arises. Let us first ask what makes an agent to act. We should note that even not acting is an act — an act of withdrawal. So, the agent has to act, but why? There are biological needs of survival; there are desires for obtaining, enjoying, consuming, recognition, influencing, controlling even those of exploiting and hurting, Besides there may be external constraints in terms of command duty, compulsion even entreaties or requests for help. The resulting effort and action, may be well planned or not planned at all. They may be explicitly oriented towards some objective or the objective may not be clear at all, in aesthetic enjoyment no definite objective can be identified. All this description can be categorized as falling in *kama* (one of the four *purusharthas*) in order to consummate an action one needs dispositional characteristics — such as motivation, observation, patience, ability and capacity acquired characteristics — such as training, skills, expertise, knowledge, information, techniques, and control; tools and instrument and their understanding; proper environment and cooperation of others. All these may be comprehended in what is called in *Gita* as *karana* means).

There are aspects of character disposition which are not centrally taken into account, but which in our present context, are extremely important. We may enumerate these aspects as, fairness, honesty, truthfulness, duty consciousness, non-coercion and concern for the other. Unfortunately, these aspects are neither necessary nor sufficient conditions for the success of an action. That is why they do not seem to be integral to action. To be fair, it is often said that honesty is the best policy. But it is not difficult to see that honesty here is subservient to some other end and so has only instrumental value. The same is true more or less about other aspects of character disposition, it is in this sense that these may form important requirements in management skills. The problem with their instrumentality is that they do not form the essence of the character of the individual and they can serve as detachable tools like other *karanas*. They are also subservient to immediate success and do not inform long-term habits.

There is another aspect of the picture, while this is a fact that in practice most of these *karanas* or means are subjugated to the success of action, there is a requirement of consistency and non-contradiction in a corporate venture. Reliability, fairness, sincerity and honesty can generate a work atmosphere in which people can work together having faith on each other. While success of action would remain the main objective the team spirit would have equal significance. obviously violence and coercion, subordination and exploitation would have no place in such a scenario.

Returning to our main problem of means and their relation to ends, we can now see that the crucial thing which is at issue is the attitude and intention which informs our effort. As character disposition they would effect our plans, our objectives, choice of our means in the wide sense as covering various aspects described above.

The choice of means imply availability of multiple alternatives. It also implies that the same objective can be attained by one method or the other. As we noticed earlier change in an state affairs can be brought about by various methods. Once we accept these propositions we shall have to look for a criterion which would enable us to choose from one of the alternative methods available to achieve a certain objective.

These considerations assume that the end attained by one or more than one alternative methods as same. This can be questioned. One of the statement of Arjuna against waging a war was "how can a bloody victory be a desirable aim?" (*Gita*, 2.5). Now the phrase in the the *sloka*, '*bhogan rudhirapradigdhan*' not only points to the '*bhoga*' but also includes the manner in which such a '*bhoga*' becomes possible "the victory soaked in blood" is victory but attained by a bloody war. The end here is being conceived as including means through which it is attained. In order to survive, it is necessary to have food, shelter and company. They can be attained by honest labour and work and they can also be obtained by unfair means — What is understood by 'unfair' would need further enquiry, while one enjoys the fruits of one's method or means one would also have in one's awareness somewhere the feeling as to now one had obtained one's objective. Fair and honest means would lend one kind of the fragrance to the enjoyment while unfair and dishonest means would stain the experience accordingly.

One might remind us that in actual experience the booty obtained by violent means hardly gives any bad feeling to the exploiter. If he or she had any unpleasant feeling attached to it he or she would have felt sorry for what he or she did and would have decided not to repeat the action again. But none of the things happen. Thus, the notion that guilt would mar the pleasure of an unfair or dishonest or cruel action is a wishful idea. This in fact is true.

Actual experience supports this objection much more than the feeling Arjuna had. But actual experience also verifies the feeling that Arjuna had. As is well known, experience does not help us in attaining a necessary relation. Examples from the experience can be cited to support any of the opposed positions. Thus the issue would be which line of thought to pursue. What should be the guidelines?

To accept the position that, doesn't matter if the objective is attained by unfair, dishonest or cruel means, it is all the same enjoyable, is to hold that unfairness, dishonesty or cruelty could be accepted as values of excellence. This obviously would be unacceptable even to those who commit to a dishonest style of life. It is a strange paradox but a fact of life that a gang of miscreants follows some rules of honesty and reliability, at least, amongst themselves.

The legendary story about Valmiki about his renunciation of

the robbery, once he realized that those for whom he thought he was committing it were unwilling to share the evil consequences of his action, shows two things. First, that besides personal gratification the motivation to an evil act is a misconceived good cause (that is, really not a good cause); and secondly, those who seem to appreciate or form a party in such actions would continue to support the evil doer forever. Each member in such a group is, normally, guided by his immediate interest and would break away from it if one finds that one's interest lies elsewhere.

These considerations lead us to think that is a logical contradiction an "inconsistency implied in an action or movement" or "structure which sooner or later create ruptures". This Marxian insight was basic to Marx's theory of social change. A group, even if it is a gang of rascals can cohere and continue to exist, so long as each member accepts some basic values — values of truth, reliability and honesty. Even a tyrant needs some faithfuls around.

Thus, it could be obvious to unprejudiced and fair mind that the choice between the types of experiences constituting an integral relationship between means and ends can only be determined by positive values.

There are some other considerations which demand attention. There are several contexts in which the means and ends do not exhibit any consonance. Bitter pills and restoration of health, punishment and correction of a wrong, telling a lie and saving an innocent life, getting soiled in cleaning something, reprimanding a child for its future career and so on. In these and similar cases means adopted seem to be in direct opposition to the intended ends.

In order to understand this problem, we shall have to go back to few paragraphs. We have distinguished between tools and instruments and the understanding of their use, certain dispositional characteristics are required for a successful action and certain aspects of character disposition which bear upon the quality of action. In cases where one seems to miss the consonance between means and ends the first two types of *Karana* hold. The act of a doctor or physician; the action of a judge or administrator, the act a teacher or a parent; the act of a well-wisher for an innocent person and so on depend for their successful culmination on the understanding of the matter, situation and individual, one deals with, one's skill and expertise and knowledge and information. But these acts are also motivated by a duty consciousness and concern for the other— the important aspects of the character dispositions. It is these characteristics that neutralize the apparent dis-consonance between the means and the ends.

In determining the proper relationship between means and the ends two basic considerations need to be taken care of : First, that means should be appropriate to ends in terms of causal relationship, you cannot reap the harvest of wheat by sowing wild seeds. Secondly, the action must conform to the basic demands of consistency and human concern. The talk of fair means will have no meaning if it is not backed by the aspects of character disposition mentioned above.

This later considerations also enable us to handle another variation of dis-consonance. Reader would remember the Sartrean notion of dirty hands. One cannot perform an action keeping one's hands completely clean–the context is social change. Surprisingly, a similar thought occurred long back in *Gita* itself. In 18.43, we are told that all actions are infected with something unwanted (*dosa*) just as fire has smoke.

Action involves the use of instruments but it also involves effort, sometimes very hardwork. In certain actions,one may have to face all kinds of hardships, even privations or sacrifices, yet such actions have in most cases, raised the ordinary human beings to a very high pedestal and serving examples for others. Such acts involved a concern for humanity informed by the values of faithfulness, sincerity, duty consciousness, fairness and devotion to truth.

Chapter – 9

Happiness—The Summum Bonum and Moral Virtue
The Construct of Emotions and Reasons

Veena Kapoor

Aristotle, in his Nicomachean Ethics, was primarily concerned with how and why a man should lead a good life to pursue his ultimate end, what is that end, and what is the nature of good life. He believed that such a moral theory should be developed which could be put into application, not only for the good of the individual but for the society as a whole. He generalized the empirical observations to ascertain that happiness could be that end which all human beings pursue. He analyzed the concept of happiness or eudaimonia by differentiating it from pleasure employed by hedonists as the *summum bonum.* He contends, "happiness is the ultimate end at which all things aim."[1] His concept of happiness is a contemplative and blissful activity having divinity, therefore, does not have hedonistic connotation. He believes that a wicked person may experience pleasantness through his bad deeds but may not be happy in moral sense. All actions, that we do, lead to some intrinsically desirable and some extrinsically desired ends. All ends are not pursued for their own sake, and he says that happiness is such an end which is pursued for its own sake.

> ". . . there is an end which as moral agents we seek for its own sake, and which is the cause of our seeking all

> the other ends — if we are not to go on choosing one act for the sake of another, thus, landing ourselves in an infinite progression with the result that the desire will be frustrated and ineffectual — it is clear that this must be the good, that is the absolute good."[2]

This ultimate end or happiness is not the state of mind or a disposition of a person, rather it is the speculative or contemplative activity for the good of the society and individual.

The goodness of a person may be articulated in terms of his attitudes and dispositions that he acquires in his repeated actions of similar kind by training his emotions through reflection. Aristotle introduced a systematic ethical theory to decide and judge the nature of actions as right or wrong. His basic intention was to know the source by which we understand the goodness or badness of actions, as we often commend or condemn persons for performing certain kinds of actions. On what basis do we judge or evaluate actions and agents? Why ought we to lead a particular way of life? Aristotle conceives goodness and badness in realistic terms, i.e., in terms of the way the good or bad people actually act virtuously or viciously. His contention was to find a relation between good or virtuous life and a happy or blissful life. He constructs a theoretical account of human behaviour and character in psychological and social nature of the agent. Through inductive reasoning we may know moral facts. For him moral goodness is that end which leads to happiness. Moral goodness has an intrinsic value and also is subordinate to happiness which he believes is an absolute and supreme end. Moral virtue is sought for its own sake; however, leads to the ultimate end, i.e., happiness.

For him practical wisdom is the source of knowing what is virtue. Our practical wisdom lies in reflecting and deliberating about practical matters of life and human relations which promote not only individual's good but of other persons as well. There are three kinds of good which determine our choices, — (i) what is pleasant, (ii) expedient, and (iii) worthy of being called good on its own account in valuative terms.[3] For (i) and (ii) we can give utilitarian explanation that those actions which promote pleasant experiences and enhance utility are good and conversely, painful, harmful and bad are the things that we shun. But in the case of factor (iii) we attribute a value which is consistently approved by all. It refers neither to the pleasant state of the mind of a person, nor to his subjective disposition, nor to the beneficial account, rather it has a reference to what can be rationally believed to be good. And he defined morally 'good' in sense (iii). According to him, social and political life should be viewed and judged by moral virtues. He contends that politicians need theoretical and practical knowledge of ethical norms and their application in human conduct. He moralized politics than politicizing morality. One cannot become a good politician just by chance or power or just by *knowing* the rules and regulations; for unless they are put into practice they cannot be proved to be good. He gives a circular meaning to virtue as he states that goodness lies in doing actions as the good actions should be done. He thought of a state which could be morally good, for goodness of an individual may be extended to the good of the society. A society is what it is, determined by the principles applied and practiced by its members. So, the way individuals would act, the sort of society they will constitute. According to him social and political life should be viewed and judged by moral virtues. To know what a moral virtue is, he believes, we require a deep understanding of emotions and their rational response to ethical and political matters which emerge as facts of human life in a society. He says :

> "For even if the good for the community coincides with that of the individual, the good of the community is greater and more perfect and both to get and to keep. This is not to deny that the good of the individual is worthwhile. But what is good for nation as a city has a higher, a diviner quality."[4]

Aristotle promotes a naturalistic teleological ethical theory. As a naturalist he defines moral concepts through empirically experienced factual concepts in scientific way. Goodness is traced in the disposition of the agent, i.e., what he does and also according to the function of the best part of soul in excellent manner. The character traits are nothing but exposition of his natural tendencies in actions under the guidance of reason. His originality lies in his coherent and systematic theory of human conduct in the light of the nature of man. He gives scientific explanation of human conduct, and his method is empirical and observational. His theoretical account of moral conduct refers to the basic principles which we use to evaluate human actions as good or as bad. Why a person acts in a way as he does? And what he ought to do? These questions need analysis of the human nature and its function, circumstances in which the actions are performed, the intended consequences, and how other human beings' interests and doer's own interests are to be safeguarded. Aristotle tried to link them together in a systematic way to give a conclusive principles for judging and evaluating human conduct. Unless an intelligible structure of moral principles is given, no evaluation or judgement is possible. The way one acts is subject to evaluation which requires the application of some fair principles commonly accepted and are contextually and rationally justifiable.

Aristotle's moral philosophy originated in the criticism of Platonic theory of absolute and eternal ideas. For Plato, the idea of good is supreme. For Aristotle good is not absolute in nature, rather it has a relative meaning based on the agent's intentions, the time, substance, quality, quantity and effects. If the agent does the action at the right time, in a right and proportionate way, in the right manner, towards the right person and is followed by desirable effects, then only it is good. Emotions and reason contribute to the decision making action in complementary and proportionate order. *Nicomachean Ethics* enquires into the purpose and goal of human life which differentiate human beings from animals and plants. The human soul (self) is represented as consisting of two parts, rational and irrational.

> "... The irrational part of the soul, like the soul itself consists of two parts. The first of these is the vegetative,

> which has nothing rational about it at all. The second is that from which springs the appetites and desires in general and this does in a way participate in reason, seeing that it is submissive and obedient to it."[5]

The connection between happiness and good life has been ascertained by Socrates and Plato also which Aristotle carried forward as an ultimate purpose of human life, but with a difference in approach.

In *Nicomachean Ethics*, Aristotle repudiated Platonic theory of Ideas and separated ethics from metaphysics. He critically analyzed Plato's concept of virtue. For Plato, virtue is a divine dispensation, and a person goes wrong in ignorance. Whereas Aristotle shows and asserts that virtue is a disposition which we acquire in the process of growth and moral understanding. For him, man is not good or bad in his initial stages. He is not virtuous by birth, he becomes so only by doing actions the way they ought to be done. Virtues and vices are learnt by self-criticism and judgements on actions by others and may be taught also. Happiness, a goal of life, can be achieved by noble or virtuous deeds, and they can be spelt in terms of practical wisdom, the *phronesis*. For Aristotle, happiness cannot be the outcome of luck, chance or cleverness. It is embedded in speculative activity. Living well and nobly pronounce the ultimate end of life, i.e. happiness. "It is happiness, say both intellectual and unsophisticated, meaning by 'happiness' – living well and faring well."[6]

Aristotle, to conceptualise the happiness as an end of human life, considers all the faculties of mind cognitive, conative and affective, i.e., desires, emotions, feelings, appetites, willingness, reason, intellect and practical wisdom in collaboration with each other. Man, being both rational and irrational, his practical discourse cannot be fully understood in the absence of either of them. Happiness can be achieved by the integration of desires, practical wisdom, reason and contemplation. The life of reason is possible only to human beings as compared to other living beings — whether animals or plants. Virtue does not imply sleeping, eating, growing or feeling, etc. The function of man should be associated with his rational nature and its authority on the irrational soul. Mitchell remarks :

> "The good of man implies excellence in his proper function and, therefore, excellence in the exercise of reason rather than in mere obedience to reason, or in a life *according to reason* rather than merely a life *accompanied by reason.*"[7]

Happiness, in Aristotle's ethics, denotes blessedness and well-being or a contemplative activity, guided by reason, for its own sake. It is self-sufficient and final end of human life, that one finds in the excellence of human nature and its function. Reason is the peculiar faculty of human soul, and human being if succeeds in excelling it in its application then only he can be happy.

> "While he calls practical wisdom consists in using knowledge, judgement, and making choices we must take account of probabilities of time and circumstances, and of individual persons. Here reason does not exist for its own sake of guidance and control of practical affairs."[8]

Thus, the happiness, the goal of human life lies in the integrated activity of speculation, desires and practical wisdom. Werner comments :

> "For Plato, contemplating eternal being is at the same time contemplating the highest good. . . The *Nicomachean Ethics*, on the other hand, does not make moral insight dependent on knowledge of the transcendental, it looks for a natural foundation of it in practical human consciousness and in moral character."[9]

For Aristotle, divine contemplative activity, i.e., happiness is the ultimate end. In human beings this divinity is very less than gods. Thus, we find, that Aristotle's conception of supreme end, i.e., happiness, is subject to be known by gods only, because they alone are absolutely virtuous; whereas man is a rational animal and is bound to act deliberately in combination of emotions with reason. Werner compares Plato's notion of Good as supreme idea and Aristotle's notion of moral goodness, that :

> "God is the measure of all things. In preserving this much from the wreck of the Idea theory. Aristotle believes he is retaining the abinding essence of Platonic morality, the notion of the absolute norm and of the metaphysical transcendence of the Good, which had given to the Platonist a new experience of God... rising at the end to the intuition of ultimate force that guides the spheres."[10]

Aristotle believes that perfect happiness is a speculative activity which is attributed to gods in their complete blessedness and felicity. Since, gods cannot be attributed concrete activities, therefore actions like justice, courage, or liberality and pride cannot be ascribed to them. He says,

> ". . . that the activity of God, which is blessed above all others, must take the form of contemplation. And from this it follows that human activities that which is most akin to God's will bring us the greatest happiness. . . the life of gods is altogether happy, that of man is happy so far as it includes something that resembles the divine activity; but none of the other animals can be properly described as happy, because they are in no way capable of speculation or contemplation."[11]

It seems that Aristotle's conception of right principle and good action can be understood in their complementary relation. Human actions are relative and perfection in them can be found only proportionately. He contends :

> "In case of human being happiness is an activity in accordance with the highest virtue; and this can only be the virtue of the best part of us that is held to have a natural right to govern and guide us, and to have an insight into what is noble and divine. . . For contemplation is the highest form of activity, since the intellect is the highest thing in us and the objects which came within its range are the highest part can be known . . . Wisdom is the pleasantest of all the good activities."[12]

Human beings, for Aristotle enjoy partially the divine nature of gods and partially irrational part of animals. Gods are involved in pure divinity and reason; whereas human beings are concerned with actions as they ought to be conducted. Aristotle believes that moral goodness is of worth only to human beings as they alone are rule-following, choice-making, judging, evaluating and deciding beings. They may do wrong intentionally or under the pressure of desires, or if desires are unregulated then they may lead to weakness of the will, or wickedness.

For Aristotle, phronesis or practical wisdom is most important intellectual virtue as a guiding principle while deciding and choosing the way to act. In *Nicomachen Ethics,* Aristotle asserts that practical wisdom is reflected in deliberations and choices made on the part of the individual. Choices regarding practical affairs are not absolutely certain and exact as they are dependent on deliberations of free and conscious agents. They do not fulfil the *wish,* but rather *will* of the agent in and through their actions. Practical wisdom is subject to the 'will' of the individual and is applicable to human decisions and choices. So practical wisdom is the prerequisite for making decisions, which dispose one to act in intended manner. Although Aristotle asserts that divine contemplation is the supreme activity, he does not make it sufficient for human beings while making decisions and choices as they are emotional beings as well. The man of practical wisdom determines the mean between emotions and acts virtuously. Moral goodness deals with feelings and actions, and Aristotle defines it as a mean between feelings in their excessive or deficient use in actions. The moderate path is sought by the virtuous or morally good man. The mean can be sorted out by a virtuous or good man by analyzing situations, other related human beings' interests and motives, context and effects of the action in advance. The mean is relative to the knowledge of human conduct. In one sense, this mean is absolute in nature, not less than the supreme good. As he states, "Goodness is one, evil is multiform."[13] Excess or deficiency can be different in degrees on various occasions, but good or the mean does not allow such a variation. Virtue or moral goodness, then, is a state of character of a human being. The choice is determined by a rational principle which commands emotions relative to human being's volitions. Aristotle says :

> "By 'goodness' I mean goodness of moral character since it is moral goodness that deals with feelings and actions, and it is in them that we find excess and deficiency and a mean."[14]

Moral goodness, in Aristotle, may be interpreted as ideals to be experienced in practical life. Virtues are norms not facts. For instance, Aristotle makes a distinction between universal justice and particular justice. Universal justice is an ideal which is pursued in concrete situations in the form of particular justice. Particular justice refers to facts gathered through experiences in spatio-temporal contexts. Werner Jaeger comments :

> "One must try to obtain conviction from reasoning, but to use the phenomena as evidence and examples. Further, it is necessary to bring the philosophical norm into harmony with the prevailing ethical views by revealing their underlying kernel of truth through conceptual manipulation. Thus, the conceptual analysis of experience replaces the soul's spontaneous knowledge of the Ideas . . . experience by itself is confused', that only the logos can lead to a clear insight in the causes of the things."[15]

Virtuous actions performed by individuals take place in concrete situations and, therefore, cannot rule out good of the individual or self-love. He says, that a man of practical wisdom or a prudent man while doing good to others takes care of his own self also. Self-love for him cannot be translated as selfishness. For him, prudence leads a man to realize his true self. The relation between theoretical and practical reason speaks for the moral virtue. Practical reason presupposes the knowledge of objective values and its application to human conduct. Happiness is the *summum bonum*, having intrinsic value to be arrived at by right conduct, or moral goodness.

Aristotle makes a distinction between three kinds of goods; external goods, goods of the body and goods of the soul. Moral virtue obviously is related with the best kind of human life. Goods of the soul are the best and more desirable and ought to be pursued for their own sake, whereas other goods should be sought for their sake rather than themselves. External goods lie outside the man himself. The rational faculty of human mind is the governing authority that judges things as good or bad. External goods and bodily goods are subordinate to the goods of the soul which lead to happiness. Happiness is a contemplative activity, some kind of wisdom. Honour, wealth, health, virtue, seems to be pursued as ends of life. But happiness is an end pursued for its own sake. Even virtue which seems to be pursued for its own sake, has a relevance if it obtains happiness. So happiness is the absolute or supreme end of the soul having intrinsic value and should be pursued by all human beings for its own sake. The Supreme good is ingrained in the best quality and faculty of human nature essentially. Human nature can be depicted in terms of its various functions and activities, and reason and intellect being the essence of human soul should be put to use and work to its excellence for the sake of which everything else exists. We may say that ". . .the life of the intellect is the best and pleasantest for man, because the intellect more than anything else is the man."[16] Wealth, good friend, good birth, good children or parents may help in achieving the ultimate end, but they are the conditions and may prove to be effective in the pursuit of ultimate end. They are not the necessary conditions. Reason, on the other hand, is the determining faculty of good actions and well-being of the human beings.

Thus, Aristotle holds that happiness depends upon the balanced and harmonious development of rational and irrational faculties of the soul. Phronesis is the intellectual virtue that gives value to life. If a man is mad then he cannot enjoy life, howsoever, he might be having health and wealth. So practical wisdom is most desirable in the practical life of man. Foolishness is to be abandoned, that proves that wisdom is the most desirable thing, as disease is to be shunned and health pursued. "Knowledge and intellect are man's true self is used there to establish the injunction that we should live for this higher part."[17] Aristotle believes that moral virtues and the actions they produce are good in themselves. Is it the actions that produce virtue or virtue produces good actions? is a trivial question to be explored. A moral theory would require both, the knowledge of the good character and its emergence. Virtue is a disposition having a reference to the virtuous person. MacIntyre echoes Aristotle's view on virtues and says, "Virtues are dispositions not only to act in particular ways, but also to feel in particular ways. To act virtuously is not, as Kant was later to think, to act against inclination, it is to act from inclination formed by the cultivation of the virtues."[18] Aristotle suggests, that "like activities produce like dispositions", so for him, one gets accustomed to perform actions time and again in a fixed way. One can know the right principle if actions of a 'sort' lead to happiness. He believes, that Absolute and perfect principles find expression in divinity of gods, but in the case of human beings it is possible only through virtuous actions. Action in itself is neither virtuous nor evil, it becomes so if it is done in the way as a virtuous person does. Virtue is the characteristic of a person, it is the human excellence that makes a man and his actions morally good. Human excellence involves person's desires, values, emotions, perceptions, interests, deliberations and choices governed by practical reason in a balanced and disciplined way. Moral goodness is expressed through desire and thought. Hudson points out, "Clearly, then, these types of character are psychological leviathans that involve intricate, interwoven, connections between desires, emotions, feelings, reasoning, perception, capacities, sensitivities and actions."[19]

Moral goodness is not merely a feeling but is the result of the deliberation and reflective thinking. Character traits, for Aristotle, are best understood in the interwoven structure of the feeling, thought and action. What one feels is due to what is thought and perceived or observed. For him, a man does not become virtuous if he accidentally acts so, he can be called courageous only when he acts as a courageous person does, intentionally always so whenever the occasion arises. Mitchell observes :

> "If Aristotle had moral "eudemonia" to denote the individual feeling of happiness of person the measure of his own good. Far from holding such a view, he agrees with Solon that one cannot safely judge the happiness of a life till after the man is dead. . . . The judgement of the worth of a life is a public judgement."[20]

A coward may at time t_1 overcome his fears and act as the courageous person does, but this does not make him a courageous person. So such good actions done by chance or once in a while do not qualify the person to be called morally good. The agent must be *conscious* of what he is doing; he must *will* his action and also with a fixed disposition, i.e., the action must be done for its own sake and must not be done for an ulterior motive. Action, done in a particular way once only, does not make a person virtuous. The virtuous person possesses virtues and exhibits them as and when are required, through actions. A virtuous person acts like a virtuous person even when he does not incline to do so. The agent must be disciplined to act in the virtuous way always. Not being able to do so is to be weak willed, i.e., not being able to fulfil one's commitments. A weak-willed person knows what ought to be done but fails to do so. Stephen D. Hudson questions :

> "Does the Aristotalian account allow that acts typical of a virtue exclude *all* reference to motivation? If so, doesn't it imply a sharp distinction between an act, as something external and a motive, as something internal? The very sort of sharp distinction that has been denied?"[21]

He resolves the issue by saying, that

> "Acts typical of a virtue acquire their value independently of how they are brought into existence. And in this sense they do not at all refer to the *motivation of the agent who* performed them. Nonetheless, I do think that what acts they are includes *some reference to motivation*; just not the motivation of the agent who performed them".[22]

We may point out here that there are many things involved while deciding to act virtuously. An agent does not become virtuous if his actions are proved to be virtuous, just or temperate merely because they have the appropriate quality. Rather, he says :

> "The *doer* must be in a certain frame of mind when he does them. Three conditions are involved, (1) The agent must act in full consciousness of what he is doing. (2) He must "will" his action and will it for its own sake, and (3) The act must proceed from a fixed and unchangeable disposition."[23]

The situation, the circumstances, purpose, and effects of the action dispose a man to act. There must be will to do and he intends to act virtuously. Hudson comments that Aristotle seems to be taking *types* of character as basic, not the *actual* agents who are found in deliberative contexts

> ". . . that principles of moral virtue takes types of agents as basic: particular acts of virtue are to be identified on

> the basis of what these sorts of agents would do. And since these principles require just the performance of certain kinds of acts, but that we *be persons of a certain type* — that we be a certain character."[24]

Does eudemonistic ethics of Aristotle has foundation in ethical egoism? Is it not the case that the pursuit of a final end is the pursuit of one's own happiness? Is not the prudence or sagacity the pursuit of self-interest? It appears that Aristotle seeks good of others while fulfilling one's own interests, i.e., good of society is preferred to the good of individual, while pursuing one's own happiness one acts virtuously which is other — regarding as well. Aristotle does not support Epicurus's view. He is not a Sophist who states that man is the sole judge of his actions. As in a playground the players play their own game but at the same time play for the whole team. There is no conflict between self-interest and benevolence. Aristotle's concept of happiness may be interpreted in terms of speculative activity having absolute value, and universal in nature. Virtue is the activity that leads to the sole end of life of any rational being. Moral goodness is not personal and private assumption rather it has a universal approach. While discussing the concept of justice, he says that man himself is not the judge of his actions, rather office will prove the man.[25] Phronesis, i.e., prudence does not rule out the reflections by others to be taken into account while dealing with practical matters . He holds that a person becomes virtuous by acting the way virtuous persons act. So, the reflections and deliberations of others are of most importance while making choices. The constituents of happiness are appropriate virtuous actions performed under circumstances and are not the private property of particular individual. Happiness, for him, is final and self sufficient end which does not require any other qualification. He clearly says that happiness is not a state of mind. It is not a psychological concept. The concept of virtue has meaning only in relation to good of the soul and the happiness consists in virtuous nature of the agent. The excellence lies in the practice, not in the concept. One who overcomes his weakness of the will can perfect his moral life. But the problem that we face in Aristotalian Ethics is how to be perfect in one's decisions and choices. Vagueness will always be there in this regard. Virtue, he suggests, is finding the mean as perfectly as hitting the bull's eye. Missing the mean implies to fall in the vicious circle. Aristotle himself says that finding this mean is a very difficult task but not impossible. We may interpret it in terms of an ideal to be pursued in the progressive order of actions.

Aristotle suggests the method of reflective and practical deliberations to make choices and judgements. Maturity, sensitivity, and understanding lead the way to know the moderate path of actions to judge rightness or wrongness. Virtue, in a sense, according to Aristotle, is explainable in terms of emotions that we put into action in an appropriate manner. Virtues deal with feelings and actions. We reflect on emotions in morality in practical and theoretical matters concerning actions. Emotions find a strong and powerful place in his morality. Emotions are regulated and controlled by their appropriation by reason, in their application in conduct. Thus, they, to a great extent, constitute human virtues and character of the individual. Thus, emotions are mental states made cognitively rich by thinking and deliberations in actions. Emotions may be divided in their expressions in the actions; and virtue refers to the appropriate degree of emotion used while doing or evaluating actions. Virtues are actualized by the motivating force of emotions in their proportionate use. Cultivated emotions in the form of virtues are the modified forms of general emotions. They no more remain faculty of mind as a matter of fact; rather they acquire an evaluative and prescriptive function. In morals, emotions have a peculiar function to perform. We do not merely give expression to emotions in stimulus-response manner, as we reflect over their use and application in actions too. Emotions are felt and experienced, in the context, to guide our choices in the future, however, they need to be regulated by reason. That is why Aristotle believes that emotions in practice can be transformed into virtues. Some vital questions need to be explained that.

> "Whether our perception of what is good (that is good as an end, not as a means) proceeds from emotion and feeling or from reason? Is human nature so ordered that we desire something as good because reason and judgement have selected it?"[26]

Sherman interprets emotions in Aristotelian ethics that they

> ". . . are about something (internal or external) that we represent in thought. As such they have propositional content. Their identity depends on that content. . . . Emotions are intentional states. As such they have cognitive content. They are identified by that content, by what we dwell on, whether it is fleetingly or with concentrated attention. Equally these states can be beliefs or just musings and construals only stenderly based on "objective" evidence. Such an account need not exclude other features of emotins, such as awareness of physiological and behavioural response or felt sensations. The claim is that these, when present are dependent on cognitive (i.e., descriptive and evaluative) content and are directed toward that content."[27]

Emotions used in moral judgements and prescriptions do not have descriptive content primarily. In virtue they have an evaluative foundation. This may be said that for Aristotle emotions in themselves are neither good nor bad. They become so when applied in a peculiar way under certain circumstances towards some kind of people. They are represented intentionally. So the emotions may be viewed and evaluated in advance, in the light of some consequences which may take place after their representation in the action. Whether they will cause harm or benefit to oneself or others is assessable in advance, to some extent. While evaluating emotion's relevance can be marked in the actions. Emotions, by themselves, do not constitute beliefs, but they are partial content of moral goodness or badness. Although emotions have an important role to play in moral judgements, yet they have to be cognized by practical wisdom. Without deliberations and reflections emotions may misguide and mislead us. Their motivational force is guarded by reason against undesirable consequences. Rightness of an action cannot depend on emotive responses alone, rather they are to be given an attentive and close look to chisel them for the desired results. Emotions have an extrinsic value for having a motivating force in the direction of one's desired moral ends. "Emotional responses are responses to intentional objects. They represent something about how we see the world."[28]

For Aristotle, emotions can be habituated in certain order through practical wisdom to constitute dispositions. These dispositions in turn dispose us to act in relation to human beings in situations and circumstances. Thus, virtues or vices are the dispositions learnt in the process of deciding and evaluating. Virtues and vices construct character by expressing our emotions and choices. And we can be held responsible for our intended emotional behaviour. Emotions can be trained to acquire patterns of actions which constitute human character. Human character is the formation of habitual actions. We get accustomed to do actions time and again in the similar order and by doing so we get hold of particular character. The sort of person I am in moral sense is recognized by the way I behave and act. It depends upon my experience and habit. Man himself is an architect of his character, and there is always a possibility of changing and mending one's ways of life. However, for an adult it is more difficult to change his patterns of actions than children. Aristotle says that by self-assessment we can improve our character. We assess others' behaviour very often, but if we evaluate our behaviour, we shall be able to identify the moral goodness with more accuracy. Appropriate emotional response shows a way to virtuous life and makes life happy.

Aristotle propounds an ethical theory that is relative and explicitly emphasizes on deliberations about the contingent and particular practical problems. Practical wisdom for him is a calculative activity and is different from scientific understanding. Any calculative and practical action is not certain and same for all times. It is relative to persons and situations. Aristotle says that all our deliberative actions are accompanied by pleasures or pains. However, pleasure and pain are not determining feature of goodness and badness of actions. For, it is pleasant to have that which a man aims at. A cheat finds pleasure in cheating and an angry man in quarrelling with others. For, Aristotle's conception of practical emotions has central place in moral virtues. Emotions have an end to pursue and one becomes pleased on achieving that end. For example anger is practiced for taking revenge. Therefore, ". . . being angry is not a matter of idle wishes. The emotion of anger is like the emotions of fear. Both are practical in the sense of involving a possible goal for which one acts."[29]

Aristotle observes and understands that courage is a virtue of good temper of emotion of anger appropriated and exhibited in response to situation while aiming at the ultimate end, i.e., happiness. That is why anger is not merely an emotion but a disposition. Aristotle observes that a person feels guilty if he does something against what he believes ought to be done and weakness of the will results. Aristotle recognizes the importance of shame as a check upon unworthy desires and cites the well-known admission of Alcaeus:

> "I wish to say something but shame restrains me'. In the *Ethics* Aristotle is equally clear concerning the restraining inference of shame. Children, he tells us, ought to have a sense of shame, for they live by emotion and are prevented from error by shame".[30]

Shame, indignation, pity and mercy are the non-practical emotions, which do not exhibit themselves in virtuous and righteous manner; they have no cognitive nature. They are not like bodily drives or non-rational appetites. Hunger, thrust and sexual desires are the class of non-rational appetites. Emotions, for Aristotle, are cognitive and, therefore, can be learnt and taught. Young people are directed to act by emotional responses and not by reasoned reflections. They learn to behave virtuously in the process of reflecting over practical matters and making deliberations.

> "Aristotle recognized that emotions are cognitive phenomena significantly different from the pleasant and painful sensations which control animal behaviour. He was in no doubt that children are emotional and, therefore, cognitive beings open to and in need of a training in values. In other words, Aristotle assigned young people an education in moral principles not in spite of, but rather because of their logical nature".[31]

Animals experience pleasant and painful sensations but they lack human capacity to make judgements, to make distinction between good and bad because they lack the capacity to think, Children have the potential to think, understand and judge, though not in a mature manner. They can learn and be taught, can analyze and understand. Animals' behaviour may be governed by pleasant and painful feelings but does not qualify for action. So animals do not qualify for virtuous behaviour, for virtue is concerned with emotions and actions. A trained and learnt emotion need not necessarily be calculated every time afresh when a person acts, for it is a disposition which disposes him to act in a relatively fixed manner. Whether an action is virtuous or not, it would depend upon the maturity with which the individual responds to the situations. The seemingly emotional response depends upon the moral character of the agent which he has consciously and willingly habituated in the course of performing actions in similar way in certain situations. Aristotle makes it sure that moral virtue makes us pursue the *summum bonum* and practical wisdom enables us to choose the right means.

Mitchell evaluates Aristotle's ethics as open to many sidedness which makes it difficult to be assigned a particular type.

> "It is *humanistic* in that it confines attention to the question of human good and finds the good for man by

> a study of the human organism, but it is *universal* in that the same method might be applied to discover the good of any type of species of organisms, or for the world as a whole conceived of as an organism. His method is *empirical* in that he begins with the observable organism but *intuitional* in that he finds the end or good by in sight into the principle of growth. The method conforms to his definition of philosophical wisdom as intuitive grasp of first principles. . . . Aristotle's theory of the good is similarly difficult to label. It is *desiderative* theory in the fact that he asserts that the good is what all men desire; and *teleological* in that the good, when known, moves men by its attraction. His theory is pluralistic in the fact that for every type of organism there is a different end or fulfilment of function and, therefore, a different good; it is *monistic* in that for the human species there is a single ultimate good. His theory of good is *objective* in that the worth of any life can be judged by other man (in fact it can be judged as a whole only after the person's death); it is *affective* in that the life according to reason is also most pleasant and enjoyable (a fact that only the subject can know since it is a matter of inner feeling). His emphasis on the character of the agent, rather than on deeds. The virtuous man not only does the right thing but does it from a rational principle, or as a man of practical wisdom would do it. It is the soul that is virtuous, not the act. There appears to be a circle here. The man of virtue is the one who is disposed to do the right thing, in the right manner, at the right time and with respect to the right persons; but the right choice is one that springs from a virtuous character, where then lies the standard of right?"[32]

Thus ethics according to Aristotle is a scientific study of human character. It cannot be classified under positive sciences. It has its own subject matter concerned with good and bad actions, and agents. Ethics as a calculative science is founded on practical wisdom, deliberations and choices consciously willed by the agent. His ethics is integrated with biological, psychological, legal, economic and socio-political values of life. He tries to show how ethics is related with other sciences. He developed a systematic and coherent theory of moral values and its relation to other sciences. He raised the problem of the ultimate end of human life and also the source and way to achieve it. The way has been shown in phronesis or practical wisdom which opens up an enquiry regarding the situations, circumstances, the deliberations and reflections made by the agent to choose, and emotions based on the desires and thoughts working together. Right choice and right action emerge from the virtue which he explains as a right action, at the right time, towards the right person, on the right occasion. The concept of virtue he acquires from Plato and Socrates but the moderate path he comes across through experience and observation in the form of habits by performing action with excellence in the union of desire and reason. In Ethics, reason for Aristotle is a distinct quality and faculty of mind in man that he can put to application in conflict situations regarding what ought to be done or ought not to be done.

The moral virtue is the state of character of the moral agent. Moral virtue or moral goodness of human excellence is highlighted in the character traits of the doer. For him the agent is praised or blamed for the sorts of actions he performs, for the upliftment of the society as a whole. Thus his approach to human relations and goodness is purposive, i.e., that action is good which is done the way a good man would do. The good man takes care of the means through which happiness, the ultimate end, is realized. For him happiness is obtainable only through the best practice of the best part of the man, and that best and peculiar part in him is reason, that guides and regulates his emotions. His character is the outcome of habits that a man develops while performing actions in the light of choices, desires, emotions, feelings, perceptions, interests, intentions to bring typical consequences of the action. So an agent becomes good by performing actions in proportionately good application of emotions under the guidance of reason so that agent and his action are evaluated as good.

We, to a great deal, may agree with Mitchell, who points out the multisidedness of Aristotle's ethics makes it difficult for us to typify moral point of view as universal or particular, empirical or intuitive, monistic — that happiness is the ultimate and, or pluralistic — that because different persons face different situations and persons; they require to find the proportionately good action. Is ethics a matter of feeling or reason? For the right principle is not given *a priori* rather is to be reflected over in the due course of time. At one state he seems to be agreeing with Plato that there is a possibility of absolute happiness which we find in speculative activity, but it can be attributed to gods. Human beings cannot experience it to such an absolute extent. Absolute happiness is the contemplative activity which is assignable only to gods. Happiness for human beings can be interpreted in terms of the pure form of pleasure that can be sought by the application of the right principle. However, this right principle may not be founded on egoism. So the principle to obtain pleasure is not self-oriented alone but other-oriented as well. At one stage Aristotle seems to be saying that good of the city – state or society is diviner than individual good. But this conception does not make his moral point of view other – regarding; rather the emphasis is laid on the good of my community my nation, my society. This sounds that, for Aristotle, the moral point of view is egoistic. On the other hand, Aristotle seems to be asserting, that good is one, to be realized by and for all generally. For him happiness is not a state of mind, nor a disposition, it is an end to be pursued by all, however, we know it through observation. His empirical knowledge cannot cross the limits of experience and generalizations. Generalizations are not absolute in nature. Therefore, can be proved to be otherwise as well. The sorts of actions in certain circumstances and among certain people may prove to be good, but may not be always so. Therefore, how can we have the understanding of virtuous actions? Virtue will differ from individual to individual, from time to time. Aristotle gives a circular account of moral goodness that lies in the moral action; and moral action lies in moral goodness. At one place he says, like activities produce like dispositions (habits) and at another he says the actions are the result of the way they are performed in accordance with certain type of actions, i.e., whether actions lead to goodness or badness; or goodness or badness refer to types of actions. Aristotle's ethical theory is a common-sense view which makes a philosophical enquiry regarding the nature of happiness and virtue in the light of human nature and his sources of knowledge.

For Aristotle, there exists a radical distinction between two kinds of knowledge, namely – theoretical knowledge and practical knowledge. Theoretical knowledge is to know and grasp and have a conception of basic principles about universal issues whereas practical knowledge is the knowledge of the good of man qua man, and a man possesses it if he acts virtuously. Practical knowledge is misconceived if applied or kept in storage as per the convenience of the person or as it suits him, e.g., a doctor might be having the knowledge about medicine but may not practice it, or may practice at his own wish. The theoretical knowledge cannot make him a good doctor. For Aristotle, a prudent or man of practical wisdom is one who makes choice consciously, willingly and in accordance with an understanding of human problems, and their retrospective consequences if reflected and practiced in certain order, and such a course of actions would articulate the *summum bonum* — the happiness, the ultimate end of human life.

REFERENCES

1. Aristotle, *The Ethics of Aristotle, Nicomachean Ethics*, tr. by J.A.K.Thomson, Penguin Books, 1952, p. 25.
2. *Ibid.*, p. 26.
3. *Ibid.*, p. 60.
4. *Ibid.*, p. 27.
5. *Ibid.*, pp. 52-53
6. *Ibid.*, p. 29.
7. Edwin T. Mitchell, *A System of Ethics*, Texas, p. 372.
8. *Ibid.*, p. 392.
9. Werner Jaeger, *Aristotle, Fundamentals of the History of the Development*, Tr. by Richard Robinson, Oxford, The Clarendon Press, 1960, p. 236.

10. *Ibid.*, p. 243.
11. Aristotle, *Nicomachean Ethics*, p. 307.
12. *Ibid.*, p. 303
13. *Ibid.*, p. 66.
14. *Ibid.*, p. 65.
15. Werner Jaeger, *Aristotle, Fundamentals of the History of the Development*, Tr. by Richard Robinson, Oxford, The Clarendon Press, 1960, p. 233.
16. Aristotle, *Nicomachean Ethics*, p. 305.
17. Edwin T. Mitchell, *A System of Ethics*, Texas, p. 237.
18. Alsdair MacIntyre, *After Virtue, A Study in Moral Theory*, Duckworth, 1985, p. 149.
19. Stephen D. Hudson, *Human Character, and Morality, Reflections from the History of Ideas*, Routledge Kegan Paul, USA., 1986, p. 43.
20. Edwin, T. Mitchell, *A System of Ethics*, p. 373.
21. Stephen D. Hudson, *Human Character, and Morality, Reflections from the History of Ideas*, p. 48.
22. *Ibid.*, p. 48.
23. Aristotle, *Nicomachean Ethics*, pp. 61-62.
24. Stephen D. Hudson, *Human Character and Morality, Reflections from the History of Ideas*, p. 50.
25. Aristotle, *Nicomachean Ethics*, p. 142.
26. Allan D.J., *The Philosophy of Aristotle*, Oxford University Press, 1957, p. 180.
27. Nancy Sharman, *Making a Necessity of Virtue, Aristotle and Kant on Virtue,* Cambridge University Press, 1997, p. 55.
28. *Ibid.*, p. 74.
29. W.W. Fortenbaugh, *Aristotle on Emotion*, Duckworth, London, 1975, p. 80.
30. *Ibid.*, pp. 80-81.
31. *Ibid.*, p. 48.
32. Edwin T. Mitchell, *A System of Ethics*, pp. 392-393.

Chapter –10

Wittgenstein's Tractatus and Remarks on Life and Ethics

A Critical Review

Dharmendra Goel

Life and ethics as generally noted do not constitute the core of Tractarian concepts as of 'Object', 'Fact', 'Proposition', 'Meaning', 'Truth' and 'Necessity' that have dominated most of his Remarks in this remarkable text. As such for last several generations of students of philosophy, Logic, Science, Linguistics and Theory of Knowledge ignore these outlandish concerns as of only marginal and expressive of his Personal Angst or only Quixotic aberrations in the enterprise of analysis, language, Mental Acts, Rules of Syntax or Semantics.

However, here, my remarks in the present Note on these Wittgensteinian themes as on life, will, value, soul, ethics, immortality and the mystical, completely disagree with a positivistic reading of his crucial Remarks in the seminal texts. While it is true that like an analytical philosopher and logician Wittgenstein would wholly dismiss the recent followers of J.L. Austin's major thesis of latter's "How To Do Things with Words" — his concept of performative utterances and ways of elucidating the commitment to act as in some situation to act specifically as having made a promise. Eminent philosophers of this persuasion such as John Searle and C.L. Stevenson and some of their followers have placed theories of "Speech Acts" and "Institutional Facts" that seem to logically coerce the speech-maker in question to adhere to obligations inasmuch as they pursue the illocutionary import (force) of their speech in the social context, it is made. For instance, when some one agrees to enrol himself as member of a club, he tacitly consents the various obligations of membership (fee, following Rules or attending meeting, etc.) Accordingly, Searle has argued this shows that some 'ought' seems to be entailed from a set of statements about 'social facts' — as person *X* consenting to be enrolled a member of a particular club, acquainting himself with relevant rules and terms relating to enrolment. The further fact is the person *X* has implicitly agreed to abide by all the rules, when he signs up. So, it is argued with meticulous thoroughness by analysis of this entire network of propositions and the presumed norms and codes clearly formulated for running such a club that once person *x* signs himself as a member, he is committed to meet appropriately the various 'oughts' that enrolment entails. For instance: Say there is the Rule that :

1. All club members pay Dues (*R*) by designated date.
2. *X* has agreed to enrol as member of this club. Therefore,
3. *X* ought to pay as dues (*R*) by the designated date. This distinction of 'Institutional Facts' as against physically brute-facts seems to dominate the speech-act analysis as initiated by Professor J.L. Austin between constative and performative utterances and later being further distinguished between illocutionary and perlocutionary acts.

Professor John Searle claims that this sort of speech act analysis, as well as his treatment of institutional facts as a species 'facts' *per se*, makes it clear that it is not impossible to deduce obligation to pay dues (*R*) by certain date logically from premises 1 and 2 as above. Of course these are involved with institutional facts.

On the contrary Searle's critics show that Premises concerned with institutional facts mask the value premises under the false rubric of so called 'institutional facts'. A sharp scrutiny can reveal and make it clear that above 1 is a pseudo-proposition in its general form, calls for following precise demonstration :

1. When properly construed shall reveal that every member such as *X* ought to respect institution's Rules such as the payment of Dues (*R*) by the designated date – It is a muted command in the garb of institutional practice. Thus construed it shall be clear that so called 'institutional facts' factual description is through and through normative and holds an implicit command with implied sanctions: So, understood and, now, adequately unpacked Professor Searle's feat of deriving 'ought' from 'is' is no more than juggler's Sleight of hand, verbally like the rabbit popping out of the hat.

What Searle's derivation of an ought from is . . . . . is no more than masking the normative obligation of paying Dues (*R*) by designated date as institutional description of club's Practices for any enrolled member such as *X*. No value has been derived as claimed from either brute or institutional facts. It is trivial masking of a command in the misleading description of the club's Practices.

2. Thus our above discussion of this celebrated Ought derivation from institutional facts preserves Value/Fact distinction, fully. Wittgenstein is categorical: No Value ever belongs to the World. World is all that is the case (See Tractatus-1). We know the whole theory of science and its method as developed in Wittgenstein elegant Philosophy of Logical Atomism (elementary General, simple and truth-functional compound Propositions) exhaustively tackles various questions of epistemology, logic and semantic analysis of science. It gives a comprehensive theory of concepts and Linguistic Meaning. Most of Tractatus is

> geared to this project to answer all problems of philosophy related to how, why, what we can think, say, mean and communicate using words and sentences putting across concepts, Propositions and arguments. It is based on simple recognition of structural Isomorphism between Signs (words and sentences) and Meaning (concepts and propositions) along with slices of reality (Objects and Facts). Our thinking uses such constructed structures out of words to constitute units of sense, elementary propositions depicting the actual configuration of facts and things of our complex world. It demonstrates, how following his theory of Truth-functional constructions science can map all the intricate structures of all that obtains in our world. Wittgenstein writes (p. 39 Tractatus 4.014) . . . . ." a gramophone record, the musical idea, the written notes and the sound waves all stand to one and another in the same internal relation depicting that holds between language and the world. They are all constructed according to a common logical pattern. . . ."

The world is a totality of facts and thus it can be expressed by means of elementary propositions; but the core of that representation is the 'logical form' present in the Thought and the world cannot be spoken of or described in any proposition although it shows itself in each elementary act of representing of a fact a configuration of objects. It shows itself but it cannot be similarly described (Tr. 4.1212. p.51 — "what can be shown, cannot be said".

As my present project does not revolve around Meaning Theory or theory of scientific knowledge to which Tractatus had made notable contributions, it suffices, here, for me to underline the demarcation between 'Facts of the World' on the one hand and their 'logical form' on the other. The latter as pointed out above cannot be asserted/spoken of, but is shown every time a fact is asserted. As for instance if we say '*Fa*' and '*Fb*', which reports that objects Tomatoes '*a*' and apples '*b*' have the same colour 'Red' as symbolised by '*F*' is the name of this object. Or say '*Fa*'. *Ra* that the tomato is red and Round. Here, we show how the same tomato occurs in our two atomic propositions as above by using the same symbol '*a*' in the two assertions, but we do not *say* it.

The seminal Ideas of Wittgenstein on fact, object, simple, name and their role in making our real world has been studied and scrutinised around the globe in last several generations of Philosophical debates. The debate demonstrates that structure of Knowledge of the world and science is centred round the theories of his elementary and General propositions. It has been succinctly argued that the mode of depicting or representing the world in language cannot be itself described; although, it is implicitly shown in every elementary proposition. As such the totality of scientific propositions that can be articulated according to the schematic procedures of 'truth functions'. The subtle logical form of language is well-captured by Wittgenstein's elucidations that if we have in the first instance two things and they are identical is nonsense and to say on one thing that it is identical with itself is to say nothing at all . . . (Tractatus, 5.5303, p. 105).

"Identity of object I express by identity of sign and not by using a sign of identity. Difference of objects I express by difference of sign" (Tractatus,. 5.53, p.105).

Finally, one must remember barring obfuscations and conundrums Wittgenstin always held: if all the elementary true propositions are given, we shall have resulting complete description of the world. The world is completely described by giving all elementary propositions and addition which of them are true and which false. . . (Tractatus, p. 63.4.26).

Having briefly put above the core of crucial world Mapping as drawn in Tractatus that holds the most elegant theory of conceptual schemes for any true Philosophy of Science and the Reality that philosophers have debated, now, feverishly over last 80 years and more, it is to further underline that the formal structure of our scientific representations as constituted by reiterated truth functional procedures of elementary propositions, that cannot be elucidated at all. This preliminary discussion should stand for the rest of my note that does not refer to logical form or issues entering truths of the world order.

3. Now, I enter into deeper issues that concern those explorations about the limits of language that cannot be talked about but are implicit in the basic function of making representation of facts. Wittgenstein's famous doctrine starts with the limits of Language: (Tractatus 5.61, p.115), it reads, "the limits of my language mean the limits of the world". "It is a startling statement to begin with. Could this suggest that Wittgenstiein's philosophy is subjectivist or solipsistic? "

First let me gather together some of the most cryptic and quoted aphorisms from the metaphysical sections of the Tractatus that of late have attracted Philosophical scrutiny across the well known philosophical facilities like phenomenology, Pragmatism, Existentialism, Hermeneutics and other newer forms of scholasticism. As noticed in the theatre of Multi-culturalism. Kuhnian Historicism Multiple-rationalism, and other radical forms post-modernism as of Michel Foucault and Jacques Derrida when some imaginative simplifiers trace these to later Post-Tractarian, Investigations and other of his posthumous MSS, now, published since 1953. It is not possible if these anti-Enlightenment Gloatings about Essentialist Reason could be traced to some kind of revisionism present in Post-Tractarian Philosophical notes of Wittgenstein, himself? Surely, he doubts early enthusiam of Viennese Circle of philosophers of Unity of Science as launched by Schlick, Carnap, Philip Frank and pursued by Tarski and Hillary Putmam in "States, Does he agree with historicists like Popper, Kripke, Kuhn and Quine who reduce philosophy into doxic conversations? Rorty, Feyerabend, Quine or Sellars: Are Davidson and others justified that there are no final criterion to prefer any of very several plausible Conceptual Schemes". Are the premonitions of Pierre Duhem and Quine truly irrefutable that scientific facts hardly provide any reliable basis to pick in between various alternative scientific conjectures as held by Popper's famous 'falsifiability criterion' after all? All conjectures are *prima facie* equally plausible as the great advocate against unity of Paradigm and conventionalism in Formal Logic of even geometries have lately argued likes of Quine and Paul Feyerabend (Against Method).

The above problematic of contemporary debtate about unity of enlightened Reason has forced people to seek support from highly subtle remarks of Wittgenstein on basic tools of thinking, conceptual necessity and possibility of articulate closed concepts and systems of unequivocal elegance. All these are highly amorphous. It is almost like a looking glass wherein hyper critical theorists see what they want to see, in later Wittgensteinian texts.

4. With these preliminary cautionary scruples gather the following gleaming of Tractatus on *themes of value*. Souls, God, mystical, Will happiness religious and the ethical that have been in my humble reading ghoulishly misappropriated by all sorts of ragtag irrationalists to buttress their pet theories. These are briefly all in the conluding sections of the Tractarian aphorisms following the above quoted remark about the Limits of Language.

"Logic should go beyond the limit of the world; for only in that way could it view those limits from the other side as well. . . . what cannot think what we cannot think we cannot say either. . . . what the solipsist means is quiet correct only it cannot be said but makes itself manifest".

The world is my world, this is manifest in the fact that the limits of language (of that language which alone I understand) means the limits of my world. (Tract. 5.62)

The world and life are one. (*ibid.*, 5.621)

I am my World (*ibid.*, 5.63).

There is no such thing as the subject that thinks or entertains ideas (Tract. 5.631).

> . . . . . if I try to isolating the subject or rather of showing that in important sense there is no subject for it alone could not be mentioned in that book—*ibid.*

For the form of the visual field is surely not like this eye (Tract. 5.6331, p.117).

Whatever we see could be other than it is there is no appropriate order of things (Tract. 5.634).

Here it can be seen that solipsism when its implications are followed out strictly coincides with pure realism. The self of solipsism shrinks to a point without extension and there remains the reality coordinated with it (*ibid.* 5.64. p.117).

Thus there really is a sense in which philosophy can talk about the self in a non-psychological way—

What brings the self into philosophy is the fact that the "the world is my World".

The philosophical self is not the human being, not the human body or the human soul with which psychology deals but rather the metaphysical subject the limits of the world not part of it (Tr. 5.641, 6-373, Tract.)—World is independent of my will. (Tr. 6.373, p. 143) .... there is no logical connection between the will and the world which would guarantee it and the supposed physical connetion itself is surely not something that we could will (*ibid.*, p.145).

The sense of the world must lie outside the world. In the world everything is as it is and everything happens as it does happen, in it no value exists, and if it did exist it would have no value. (*ibid.*, 6.41). . . . if there is any Value that does have Value, it must lie outside the whole sphere of what happens as it is the case. . . for all that happens as is the case is accidental. It must lie outside the world (Tract. 9.145).

So it is impossible for there to be propositions of ethics (*ibid.*, 6.42) propositions can express nothing that is higher (*op. cit.*) it is clear that ethics cannot be put into words (*ibid.*, 6.421, p. 147) ethics is transcendental (ethics and Aesthetics are one and the same) (Tract. 6.421).

> .... doubt can exist only where a question exists, a question where an answer exists and the answer only where something can be said (*ibid.*, 6.51, p.149).

The solution of the problem of life is seen in the vanishing of the problem (*ibid.*, 6.521).

(Is not this the reason why those who have found after a long period of doubt that the sense of life became clear to them have then been unable to say what constitute that sense?) *ibid.*, 6.521.

There are, indeed, things that cannot be put into words. They make themselves manifest. They are what is Mystical (Tract. 6.522). an ethical law is of the form 'thou shalt. . .' is laid down. One's first thought is, 'and what if I do not do it'? . . . ethics has nothing to do with punishment and rewards in the usual sense of the terms . . . so our questions about the consequences of an action must be unimportant at least these consequences should not be events. . . there must indeed be some kind of ethical reward and ethical punishment, but they must reside in the action itself.

(and it is also clear that the reward must be something pleasant and the punishment something unpleasant), Tr. 6.422., p.147)

If the good or bad exercise of the will does alter the world, it can alter only the limits of the world not the facts not what can be expressed by means of language.

In short, the effect must be that it becomes an altogether different world. It must, so to speak, wax and wane as a whole- the world of the happy man is a different one from that of the unhappy man. (Tract. *ibid.*, 6.43).

So too at death the world does not alter but comes to an end (*ibid.*, 6.431) death is not an event in life. We do not live to experience death if we take eternity to mean not infinite temporal duration but timelessness, then eternal life belongs to those who live in the present. *Our life has no end in just the way in which our visual field has no limits* — (Tr. 6.4311 — underlining, here, is mine, and not Wittgs).

The temporal immortality of the human soul, that is to say of its eternal survival after death. . . fails to accomplish the purpose for which it has always been intended. Or is some riddle solved by my surviving forever? Is not this eternal life is much of a riddle as our present life? The solution of the riddle of life in space and time lies outside space and time (6.4312 Tr.)

How things are in the world is a matter of complete indifference for what is higher. God does not reveal himself in the world (6.432) "It is not how things are in the world that is mystical but that it exists" (Tract. 6.44) to view the world sub-species aeterni is to view it as a whole — a limited whole — feeling the world as a limited whole — it is this that is mystical (*ibid.*, 6.45, Tractatus) when the answer cannot be put into words neither can the question be put into words — *The riddle* does not exist.

If a question can be framed at all, it is also possible to answer it (Tract. 6.5).

We feel that even when all possible scientific questions have been answered the problems of life remain completely untouched, of course there are then no questions left and *this itself is the answer*. (Tractus 6.52, p.149 — Underlining here is not Witt.'s). It need to stress the following thesis on 'subject' as under: "*The subject does not belong to the world: rather, it is a limit of the world* (*italicised* mine. *op. cit.*, 5.632). It is important to remember what Tract. 5.5423 says about the way we see as complex figures that is comparable to the concept of seeing as introduced in later Wittgenstein's philosophy of post-investigation variety like his Puzzle pictures of Duck and Rabbit or the contrasts of foreground and background in seeing Rubens' Vase. This should be illustrated :

There is no doubt, it also explains why there are two possible ways of seeing the figure as cube; and all similar phenomena. For we really see two different facts. . . Another important scaffolding of our explanatory devices that show how our perspective of conceptual networks are bases of alternative models of explanations ". . . . *The different nets correspond to different systems for describing . . . . just as with the number system we must be able to write down any number we wish. So with the service of mechanics we must be able to write down any proposition of physics that we wish*" (Underlining mine. *Ibid.*, 6.341).

". . . Laws like the of sufficient reason, etc., are about the net and not about what the net describes" (*ibid.*, 6.35)

Lastly Wittgenstein completely doubts the justification of

uniformity of nature/ induction. . . He categorically holds "*the whole modern conception is founded on the illusion that the so called laws of nature are the explanations of natural phenomena*" (italicised mine. *op. cit.*, 6.371) preceding it . . . . we read (Tract 6.37) *There is no compulsion making one thing happen because another has happened. The only necessity that exists is logical necessity (Tract. p. 143 italicised mine).*

5. *Critical observations on Wittgenstein's Analysis of 'The Subject', 'Value', 'The Free Will', 'Ethics' and 'The Mystical'.*

Now, onwards, here, we would bring out the implications of the preceding aphorisms from his Tractatus to give an overall perspective that has often not been adequately delineated so far by his numerous critics and other specialized words, that get multiplied by dozens every semester, round the globe. The very diversity of such interpretations from Existentialist's, Phenomenologist's on the one hand and possibly some tracing Vedantic and Buddhist similarities (amongst asian students) to Pragmatist's, Post-Modernist's, Kuhnian and other historicist's, Multiple-Rationalist's conventionalists on the other. I do not wish to dispute their right to seek confirmation of their own pet standpoints. I see as there could be some grain of truth for such a reading of his aphorisms, but, I can say that such an exegetic debate can be very dreary and protracted without any conclusiveness.

As such, let me begin here with the crucial account of 'The Subject' as we have already gathered the relevant aphorisms, earlier. To the best of my skill I seek to build his views on "the non-object" view of the subject as it is shown to be the limit of the world. (*ibid.*, 5.632, 5.633 and 5.633.1). It is, maintained that Wittgenstein in these aphorisms starting 5.631 demonstrates that any thing like Soul, substance. Being psychic entity or Mind stuff as often hypostatised or analysed by Neuro-Scientists, Brain theorists, logical-behaviourists or in debates on Consciousness, Mind-Body relation is radically mistaken and should be disposed of. In no way can the subject be part of any Object of configuration of objects that are put across in our 'World-Perspective' showing his theory that the constitutive 'Eye' that puts across the field, can in No sense be a part of the field (figure of field as a limited whole; *ibid.*, 5.631 is thought as pivotal to Wittgenstein's rest of the Analyses of Metaphysical self that could not be in any World made of objects and yet as he argues 5.62 a little earlier that the World is *My* world. . . the limits of my language mean the limits of my World. He demonstrates how solipsism is quite correct only it cannot be *said*. See following 5.621— The world and Life are one). What is asserted by the present observation on these recondite aphorisms that in their beguiling simplicity. They stand a very radical vision of "The Non-Subject" as the very constituent pre-condition of any possible World. Things, Facts, Objects and their various configurations presuppose the overall visual Field mentioned above wherein these are founded but no self could be logically located in this field as just now demonstrated it is the Transcendental presupposition of *'My World'*. It is easily the metamorphosed thought of Kantian Epistemology (Remember Wittgenstein did read and quoted Kant in the Tractatus) — the idea of Original Transcendental unity of apperception — of course a transcendental mouthful but very logically demonstrable pre-condition of any possible representation of Worldly Phenomena. I must add what I learnt from our teacher Professor Anukul Chandra Mukerji at Allahabad University in 1950s that no one should commit the fallacy of Transcendental Dislocation by conceptualizing the Original unity of Self as an object in the World. In analogy to classical Advaita theory of *atman*, Mukerji would say that it is *adhyasa* that misapplies categories of world Making to the very transcendental presupposition of any possible world (See, Self, Thought and Reality, Indian Press, Allahabad, 1952). So be it, Wittgenstein in this very scenario reformulates in his own brilliant innovation that the limits that belong to the projection by our Eye for the field cannot include the constituting Eye, itself. That would be putting the horse before the cart.

One can also mount like many later day Phenomenologists who follow Edmund Husserl's theory of Intentionality claiming *a priori* Self as the noetic condition for positing any Noematic affirmation that is claimed to represent some content in our intentional act. Well, these are colourful analogies, and possibly elaborate the rich implications of Wittgenstein's "Non-Object" sense of the Constitutive Subject of any possible 'My World'. However, like Kant and unlike *Advaita* or perhaps even Husserl, Wittgenstein has no weakness for reifying this purely logical limit into a Metaphysical Identity that is the essence of the World. . . . We should realize how the Kantian critique of Metaphysical Dialectic shows that by illegitimate use of categories of Understanding only ends in Metaphysical Antinomies like a metaphysical free Agent as well as fully determined Mind being part of the Natural Order. So, Wittgenstein is above any such metaphysical chimeras. We can only change the limits of the world by our Vision but nothing of those facts that it is made of. We can see 'Facts' as demonstrated by Wittgenstein in Tractatus-Investigations and Remarks on the Foundations of Mathematics that the conceptual Nets (Tractatus. 6.341 already by quoted here above) could see the world and universe only through them but these cannot in any way be any part thereof. The world is all that is the case, it is ultimate in realism that remarks like 'I am My World' (5.63 & 5.64 Tract.). It must be realized that Wittgenstein despite appearances had stayed to be a philosophical Realist: even when, he was showing "Truths" of conceptual limits that are inborn to our language, No Metaphysics.

6. *Naturalistic Fallacy, Form of Life, Language, Games, Later Wittgenstein*

It is important to face the myth that Philosophical Investigations supports cultural relativism, as it dosowns Tractarian Foundationalism and underlines 'Form of Life'. Multiple Rationality as marked by his doubts of about so called laws of thought including the challenged Law of Excluded Middle by intuitionist accounts of proofs and possible conventionalism of Axiomatised Proof Theory as Brouwer and Weyl in basic Mathematics and Kuhn and Feyerabend in the other physical Sicences and their historical developments have laboriously worked out in last several decades, this happened since his posthumous publication of Investigations. As I have picked up some of these issues related to logic Science, 'limits of speakability' in my other notes that may be published soon (Forthcoming issues of *Bihar Journal of Philosophical Research*, now) I cannot detain myself to the luxury of reviewing these debates here, and offer my humble views on these disputed questions. In so far the bearings of these questions can be recognised on Wittgenstein's views on Mind, Values, Freedom of the Will, Personal Identity and Moral Life. It is my contention that Wittgenstein totally rejected popular cultural social predeterminism and socialization about these persons. Her values or Agent's self determination by means of cultural and social positioning and Ideology. This is grossest form of crude reductionism that completely and totally misunderstands the autonomy of the person and her capability to constitute her own 'Limits' that only generate her World as emphasized in earlier parts of this note. What Wittgenstein clearly draws us out to see that anything that belongs to our World or any of its 'Facts' can have no Value, what is the case, repeatedly (*op. cit.*, 6.432 ff) He says, ..."the sense of the world must lie outside. In the world everything is as it is and everything happens as it does happen: in it no Value exists *and if did exist, it would have no value*... any value that does have value, *it must lie outside the whole sphere and is the case* What makes it non-accidental cannot lie Within the World. *Since if did it would itself be accidental"*. . . . (Understanding the underlined aphorism makes his Views on Values crystal clear and prove his doctrine as Non-naturalistic — *ibid.*, 6.41).

So, whatever, strenuous consensual theories of acculturation, self construction and social predeterminism and cognate sciences may strive for Wittgenstein these are all vulgarised forms of naturalistic fallacy that psychological Hedonism and utilitarian social sciences have always espoused without either understanding the role of human conscious repressentation of World and the Man's place at very genesis of the Field that goes to make the different 'Facts'. According to his view, if we have any Value it is only in our mode of seeing the world as a Limited whole that gets formed owing to the 'limits' that we put on this created perspective, which is our own creation. In that sense Person who is Happy or Unhappy has entirely due to different 'limits' that either uses to create these two 'Limited Wholes'. (See *op.cit.,* 6.43 and ff 6.431) The entire existence of Person, these 'Limits' and the Perspective of the limited created totality begins and ceases together. They are coeval. The world so constituted cannot be derived from the various commutations and combinations of these elements, themselves that are placed in our field, of grasp by our. 'Form of life'. Swaly, not for nothing had he said as we mentioned "*We, our life and our World* wax and wane with our envisioned values. When we cease, nothing, alters in world of Happenings but the "World that we inhabited" just ends."

Wittgenstein was a radical thinker who refused to be ruled by Either Enlightenment theory of Utilitarianism or social determinism, Darwinism and psychologisms such most ethical rationalism advocate. We know how great strides of Brain-Research Behaviour Therapy, Psycho-Analysis, Identity Theory have glibly theorised that we are creatures of Ecology and social conventions and our Persona itself, is only an emulation of words and Symbols that are bombarded on us in our maturation, which we ourselves mimic and start seeing ourselves as the created person whose percepts, Motivations and Character are thus reflexively constituted almost like our Destiny.... Wittgenstein would reject such incorrect analyses of our natural History as perverse and completely unconcerned with the process of our self-sculpture including Values and our Will. He has with clarity shown time and again that such a simple thought as "7 + 5 is equal to 12" cannot be reduced to any neurological events that could be spirited away from our brains by the devices of Neuro-Science (See Blue and Brown Books). The sight of my brain events as projected before my eyes on the Screen are not in any way the same as concept / idea of the simple numerical truth. Much effort no doubt is being launched by writers like Minsky, Penros Daniel Dennet, Piaget, Eccles, Penfield, Sapir, Konrad, Levy Straus to explain Man's Individuation though ongoing conversations and cultural internationalisations of societal practices, etc. But do these Views get to the creative role constitutive Perspectives we generate that, we alone and alone forge and posit as 'our world'? Wittgenstein would argue no never anything these reified 'facts' as variously drafted by Social Science could ever intersect what essentially is transcendent of any finitary, doings, happenings that such empirical studies mobilize and wrongly hope to map the Freedom of the Moral Person. We must note as noted earlier (*op. cit.*, 5.631 Tr.) the world as I found it, "I should have to say include a report of my body, and should have to say which parts were subordinate to my will and which were not, etc. (here, it, is important to refer to Aristotelian classification of reflexive, involuntary and voluntary and his Praxis as science of Motivation or causative Praxiology, how, much enriched by several sharp distinctions drawn by our contemporaries amongst Intended/ Unintended. Proximate/remote, spur of the moment get decisions deliberately meditated, well-calculated self-conscious." Decision and others the stock-in-trade of analytical Social Science theory, (Merton, Maslow, Freud . . . Konrad, Jung, Adorno) . . . "this being the method of isolating the subject for it alone could not be mentioned in the Book" *(ibid.*, Tractatus). The claim that was made by this note is supported by the above aphorism relating to the view that there is no Subject who interacts with the ways of parts of the World. Self, Person: Agent are only logical Limits of my World as underlined by this exploration into the Agency and its analysis by Wittgenstein.

Briefly, once again, the entire discourse of Logical empiricism under the leadership of well known philosophers of Post-Philosophical Investigation's period marked by "Ghost in the Machine" anathema by Rylean concept of Mind. Ayer, Davidson seek to translate the Mental Predicates in terms of physical predicates or the computer savvy Minsky and Dennet putting the two discourses about mental-acts/ functions in the other discourses of observable neural and singular or compounded Brain-Functions, without residue. Lately, Neurological Sciences coupled with cognitive sciences hope to give comprehensive explanations of all mental discourses to the minimal objective dispositions of hard data about our neuro-physiological events and translation programmes to devise equivalences of First person self-conscious reports into relevant Third-Person arrays of neural events. Obviously here once again while Wittgenstein was such a primary initiator of linguistic turn of twentieth century philosophy he would simply reject the entire conceptualization, reductionism and hubris of seeking identification of self-conscious first person immediate Grasp of Value. Personal identity and willed Intention as mixing space-time events of our World that are put across only by our Field-Vision itself only within the limited whole that is there in the intended Act of my World (*ibid.*, Tract., 5.633 and 5.633.1).

Having thus disposed of the most celebrated theories of analytical philosophers and committed social empiricists it is to underline what Wittgenstein has to disagree with the enlightenment thesis of inductive Sciences and their famous Law models applicable to natural, social and life worlds. He characterises these fabulous prejudices as entirely unwarranted prejudices. Takes the radical empiricist position of Hume that logically there is no justification for our expectation that Sun will rise in the east tomorrow as it has been noted to do so many times in our individual and collective memory. He writes: "what can be described can also happen; and what the law of causality is meant to exclude cannot even be described" . . . *ibid.*, 6.362. This procedure, however, has no logical justification but only a psychological one— *op. cit.*, 6.363.1.

"The world is independent of my will" (Tract. 6.373). It shows how far too deep chasm falls between our will of the wisp Wishes that Wittgenstein underlines, that no future of inductions can cure. We live in the perennial uncertain, contingent, congeries of Facts, happenings Events that do not fall under any necessity to conform to our desires or hopes. Having thus cured, ourselves, of Divinity and Moral redemption metaphysically, that is, if we express our

Moral Values we ought to be clear it is our Choice, and our Freedom and a product of our own existential perspective-rooted in our First Person awareness of that which 'we see' as the defining limit of my World. So, the World is under No obligation to realise our fond dreams. Here, Wittgenstein crosses over from religious Moralists, Vedantins and Christian Faith healers, completely, and almost entirely supports Sartrean Theory of radical disjunction of 'me', 'my World' and 'the others'. Yet as one condemned to be free to make my World my own, it is me and me alone who commits with open eyes without false hopes.

Wittgenstein may not quarrel much with his teacher G.E. Moore on the latter's Characterization of Personal Freedom in his concise refutation of self-determinism of the Agent's Choice despite given all the details of one's biography, physiology and social milieu as Moore holds "I could have done Otherwise" — on precisely the bases a person comes to have a new orientation on the given facts any time, if he does have that or not is a mystery that cannot be pierced or premeditated that is the riddle of existence *per se*. As such in the life of Spirit nothing is ordained beforehand and each person is a radical mystery that cannot be derived beforehand from genetic, economic, social or any power data-bases as liberal or Marxist social scientists would like to expostulate.

Likewise, Wittgenstein would side with much of Kantian Transcendental approach to Moral Freedom as adumbrated in his Second critique as the Moral Agent is not subject to causal nexus of phenomenon of the experienced world. Kant's theory of categorical Duty and total indifference of empirical consequences of pursuit of moral Value is in conformity Wittgenstein's account of the entirely non-empirical dimension of Subject, Persor. His World making foundational vision and associated pursuit of Values and their realizations or failures, which incidentally do not in anyway affect that validity. It is enough that a person authentically has the given Value-Perspective whether it leads to specific consequences is in principle impossible on the analyses of the disjunction that Wittgenstein's ideas of Values as Transcendental imply.

There is little left now to say about persons and their freedom as visualized in Wittgensteinian perspectives on the nature of Limiting Perspectives that our interpretations of his aphorisms imply on the context of 'I' making my own "World". I only remark that lately P.F. Strawson in his work *Freedom and Concept of Resentment* has resiled away from the analytical regimen of his earlier reductionist programme of M-Predicates to P-Predicates. Now, he seeks to offer a liberal reconciliation with his non-reductionist theses of what he recognises as 'Compatibilism' between hard core third Person Scientific Discourse that logical behaviourist have long advocated and the contents of First person Singular and Unique Body of Beliefs that demand respectful attention from all philosophers who wish to propose to appreciate Human-Condition in all its richness. The question that Wittgenstein would offer to appreciate that unlike Strawson and others of their Analytical dispositions could give up putting weighted preference for the third Person discourse; while Wittgenstein would not be least willing to concede any canonical order in creating any hierarchy of different Language Games. (See p. 1)

7. *Wittgenstein on the concept Rules and their Applications — "Others Pursuit of Possibly Shared Values"*

Before closing the present note on these neglected themes of Wittgensteinian aphorisms, I want to take note of his very critical analyses that these offer relating to overcoming 'Singularity' in his picture of Human Condition. While he strongly valorizes first Person Singluar's perspective on One's own Values and how his sharing them if at all possible with others. We all know that Wittgensteinian remarks indulge in mutually seemingly contrarian features of his views on the existence of others. We can refer to logical howlers that he always rejoiced wherein he seems to show the impossibility of someone ever knowing that how other is in some or the other mental state such as 'pain'. What is the criterion to apply that we can be sure that the bodily attributes that we reckon are not really put up, i.e., he is that pretending related with this issue concerns logic of conceptual usage that such Agent-Centric mental states could ever be open to access to others? If so, How? The other side of this vexed controversy relates to crucial thesis of Investigations (Note 246 FF). That there cannot be any Private Language. The strong thesis of "No Private Language" simply underscores his analysis of Rules and their applications in order to either understand ever What a Sign, Word, or a token can convey. The entire gamut of Language Games, Use Theory of Meaning, Discourse organisation that our mental life offers is based on the Public scrutiny of Criterion and demonstrability of its violation in use of any sign or its articulating concept with other signs. No meaning could be articulated if the Rules, Criterion and their applications are not governed by unequivocal intelligibility conditions. It is only strongly demonstrated by extensive review in Philosophical Investigations of Ordinary Usage that every possible assertion priorly fulfils the finitary intelligibility requirements under which alone they could make sense. (I have as mentioned, before, done another study of these constitutive Rules in his theory of Language-Games. See Post-Modernity and Wittgenstein, etc. in B.J.P.R.) The only amendment that later Wittgenstein envisages in widening the scope of intelligible Discourse to include for those assertions whose truth conditions are not feasible but where necessary intelligible cluster of words do not violate the logical Grammar. If they do not, then, these could both be asserted as well could be intelligible. Such a proposition. Say, '*5 is equal to three added to Two* is true at Hours in the Morning "violates the intelligibility conditions of both the concepts of numbers like '5', '3' and '2' as well as the conceptual Structure of the 'true proposition', Whatsoever. For consider a temporal description like 'john reached his home at 4 p.m. shall continue to be true and cannot be only true at any specific Hour after once the report has its truth conditions realized, as asserted. Just as, it does not make sense to claim that our report is true only for friends and relations, either. The whole articulation of the Form of life very often not properly grasped by populist social theorists create such abominations and logical fallacies, violating the natural topology of our natural History of Ideas. So far from the way Kuhnian and Feyerabendian relativism has captured the Language Game-concepts and assimilated them into their own confused talk of Paradigm-Shifts. Wittgenstein's views have been largely distorted by even Great logicians like Saul Kripke who wrongly assimilated the Criterion of 'rule following' to be governed by the majority vote of those who are users, if in any specific case, a rule is observed or violated. I think this is incoherent mode of rendering Wittgenstein's Game Theory calls for Following Correction.

Briefly, there are several strands and braids in the proper handling of the concept of Rule following: We must ask and get these strands fully separated before we gather unequivocally how Wittgenstein used the metaphor of Game to give a model of Language use.

1. What Are The Actual Locutions That Express The Rule In Question.
2. We Must Make Sure What The Rule Stipulates In Terms Of Application.
3. We Must Make Sure That We Get The Rule Content Unequivocally.
4. We Make Sure That We Identify The Right Domain Of Instances To Which It Applies.
5. Finally, We Enumerate The Set Of Instances That Produce The Outcome Of The Correct Application Of Priorly Fixed Content Of The Rule.

All these steps could be mismanaged and could lead to misapplications of the Rule/criterion and produce Ambiguous Domains. Wittgenstein's later parts of ordinary Language Game theory is replete with rendering these vagueness and open textured character of our world Makings. Remember the indeterminate demarcations of colour Words, at ends of Blue and Green and intermediatory shades as in his own coinage 'Grues' and 'Bleens' — we for sure cannot eliminate difference, here, in seeing sets equivocally and some person calls something Blue which others on the basis of his finer colour discrimination sees it is Bleen or Grue. . . So there is the limit to public correction, and it remains open-textured to stipulate the specific colour Patch even by application of a colour Sample or our own eidetic Memory. It is shown that the same person calls two different identical samples to belong to different shades and two different samples the same name, i.e., says Blue. Likewise, two persons generate different application of one and the same Rule because they understand it as being two different rules, consider the remarks from Wittgenstein's Work on Foundations of Mathematics: he argues about the rule of generating an odd number series like 1, 3, 5, 7... and so on yet, some one more resourceful sees this principle to be a more difficult rule having the strain after reaching No. 99 to mean onwards 103, 107, 111. . . and still a third reading that after 1001 reaches out to mandate 1007, 1015, 1023. . . and so on. In initial conditions of the sequence the three identities of the rule, here, have the same application but later they have different sets that differentiate them from each other. Likewise, let us say in Tennis the Service must not get under the net. But how high over the net? say 10 cms, 200 cms or 100 metres very obviously very few rules could be entirely free from vagueness and have strict correct application and we see this in legal battles everyday. So, since all of us imagine our identities in terms of inbuilt identification rules and their axiomatic non-ambiguity we are led into confused alley of mixed up identities even while we claim to know our own memories best, and if not so who other would know better? A saman, A psychiatrist or the Magistrate empowered to certify it by Law? There is accordingly all sorts of misapplications yet we are in a position to manage our relations in the world by muddling through.

We all know our identities are imagined fables that play such a crucial role in creating our "Selves". For a fact, now, most shall agree that what to speak of Memory based Psychic Identities even our Physically tangible somatic identity is under permanent reconstruction, reminiscent of Artistotelian problematic of how the same ship continues when it is being step by step, plank by plank, getting replaced with newer sails and decks and different configurations of decks and berths. . . "Is it not like Nagsen's chariot or Ryle's Onion Peels that when stripped, we are left with only void". Shades of Buddhist Anicca, Anata, Anattma. Yet we are Non-object Self. True, we are creatures of our own vijnapattis. An illusion within an illusion without being a religious person Wittgenstein did say that world exists is itself mystical . . . further — that it is "feeling the world as a limited whole — it is this that is mystical" (Tr. 6.45) We achieve timelessness like the field vision of the field of our seeing horizon and by not everlasting through Space-Time. All doubts are set aside when we realize the world, things, thoughts all flow from our own vision rooted but never seen at the base of our world. We are thus led into Eternity through such recognition of our own projections of our World-Making. To know this is not to know that we have solved any Value Riddles or World's socially engineered metamorphoses. We have seen the vanity of such illusions and realize that in the dumb furniture of contingent objects we are ourselves the chit. Light and illumination that reveals its myriad mysteries and as we know, we have solved all the riddles, that-then we pass out in silence.

Buddha said finally, *Atma Deepo Bhava* — Be lamp to yourself, and you shall be liberated of accumulations of nescience Final Word. Archytus commenting on his formidable Teacher Heraclitus who held that no one can enter the same river twice... to have added his own sharp gloss "Sir not even once . . . for between the thought and the action falls the shadow. . . . there can be any number of slips between the cup and the lip. . . . and so on".

So, as Wittgenstein argued when these solutions are seen in the way they are meant, then no questions remain and all doubts for fact end. We must pas out in silence.

Chapter – 11

Nowells Smith's Multifunctionalism

Pratima Ganguli

Among the post-emotive thinkers Nowell-Smith is one whose name will ever shine in the history of moral philosophy. In his famous single work *Ethics*, first published in 1954, he very explicitly and elaborately covers a vast field of moral problems which was not touched by any of his emotivist or post-emotivist predecessors. Prof. Hare very rightly remarks while reviewing the book *Ethics* that "Mr. Nowell Smith is a fox, not a hedgehog; he covers a wide range, and says a great many sensible things, rather than a few momentous ones".[1]

Like Hare, Nowell-Smith rejects ethical Naturalism as well as Intuitionism as he too supports non-descriptivism in ethics, and advocates the view that ethical language is primarily action guiding. His approach to ethics is unique and novel in its own way. He laments that "The study of ethics seems to end in a blind alley".[2] He was not satisfied with the trend of older philosophers and also with Logical Positivist's or Existentialist's approach. He believes that the traditional philosophers have only tried to find out what the good life is or what our duties are. But they never succeded in reaching the goal. The later philosophers, namely, the Intuitionists, also failed to lead us to the goal. Curiously enough they have offered us an exciting short-out road (i.e., immediate insight) which only could be able to lead us to Scepticism.

Regarding the views of logical-positivists, Nowell-Smith, like many other philosophers, believes that they completely deny the possibility of moral knowledge. Similarly, the existentialists according to Nowell-Smith give extreme freedom to human beings and deny the authority of scriptures and believe that morality is determined by the complete freedom of human desire. This too is to some extent an extreme position regarding moral matters according to Nowell-Smith.

Nowell-Smith, on the other hand, very rightly has tried to save the situation. Let the existentialists lament that their freedom is being sacrificed at the altar of reason. But he propounds his moral theory mainly on rational base. Although the other post-emotivists, whom we have discussed in our previous chapters, do recognise the role and importance of reason in ethics, it is a pity that their theories recognise only one kind of rational role to the language of morals and that also in a defective way . So far, we have been told that ethical statements are the expressions of feelings or else they evoke the name in others, or that, they are of the nature of imperatives or again, more liberally we may say, they are action-guiding.

But Nowell-Smith does not admit any single function of moral judgements. Choosing and advising are the two main functions of moral langugage according to him.Not only this; he believes that ethical languages have variety of uses.They can be used to express taste and preferences.They can also be used to criticise, to express decisions, to evaluate, to praise, to encourage and so on and so forth. He further points out that we have to find out the connections between these functions. In this own words "These activities form the complex web of moral discourse and our problem is to trace the connections between them and to come to understand how; it is that the same word can be used in all these different ways."[3] It is for this reason that Brandt calls Nowell-Smith's theory as "Multi-functionalism".[4]

Nowell-Smith holds the view that the use of logical language in ethics is the root cause of every confusion.There are certain assumptions which belong to logic only, and ethics has been made unintelligible by their use in its range. More often, the logicians assume that all adjectives play the same role, i.e., stand for a property. Against such a view, Nowell-Smith raises the question "Do all adjectives stand for properties?"[5] In course of his discussion, N. Smith lastly answers that moral adjectives do not stand for any properties. According to him the above confusion is based on two kinds of bias. In the first place, we generally use to believe that empirical adjectives are the names of properties, which denote or refer to or stand for something we just as in "The mercury is liquid" the adjective is the name of the actual property that the metal mercury possesses. Secondly, we use to ask "What does the word mean ?" but Nowell-Smith thinks that this is a wrong way of asking. Rather we should ask according to him "What does so and so mean by the word ?"[6] A word does not mean anything by itself; it is we who mean something by the word. We have every right to mean anything by a word.

On the basis of the above two grounds, Nowell-Smith again turns up to a question which he thinks as the most important one in ethics and upon which the place of his ethical theory is built up. The questions is : "Is goodness a property" We have seen that according to him adjectives do not stand for properties. He further believes that moral adjectives such as 'Good', etc., also do not stand for any property. Now we will see how in his own way Nowell-Smith gives the answer to the above question.

"Is goodness a property ?" is a difficult question to be answered. We can simply give the answer by showing similarities and differences between 'good' and other adjectives. More practically adopted this method by making a comparison and contrast between 'good' and 'yellow'. He lastly reached the conclusion that good is a non-natural quality whereas yellow is a natural quality. The distinction between natural and non-natural quality accordingly was based in the notion that while the former belongs to spatiotemporal relation the latter is beyond that. But this vague word 'non-natural' did not impress any of the later philosophers. And they thought it to be correct to define 'good' as a gerundive property, which implies 'should' or 'ought'.

But Nowell-Smith proceeds a step further when he says that gerundive properties are not properties at all. They are simply some mental reactions. We have discussed above that good is neither simple indefinable non-natural property, nor any complex whole too. It is not meaningless also. So the questions naturallya rises 'what is is' All these discussions create problems according to Nowell-Smith, only if we believe that adjectives are the names of properties which denote, refer to and stand for something else.

He argues that all meaningful words are not the names of things; meaning does not imply naming. There are some philosophers who use to think that all words are the names of what they mean. They presuppose that meanings have those characteristics that a thing must have in what we call the name-thing situation. Let us take the example of the word 'Wall'. It certainly refers to a thing wall, which is an objective fact. And we can very well perceive this thing, i.e., the wall, with the help of empirical observation. In the same way a group of philosophers, i.e. Institutionist, consider that moral words are also the names of things which refer to non-natural objective properties and which we perceive through inward observation, i.e., Intuition. But, Nowell-Smith believes it to be wrong and remarks "Mearings" come to be regarded as indefinable individuals which crop up every now and again, as distinct and self-identical as the boys in a class".[7] This situation, Nowell-Smith believes, leads us to a further consequence and makes philosophers ask the questions "what do word mean?" Let us suppose *'P'* is a word. In one situation it may mean *'R'*, as it performs the job in another *'S'* and in a third one it can equally mean *'T'*, as it performs the job *'T'* and so on. Now, in this situation we may face the problem as to how to explain the word *'P'* ? If the word means the same thing in the same context, then what will be the meaning of the word *'P'* ? In the above situation the word *'P'* sometimes means *'R'*, sometimes *'S'* and sometimes *'T'*.

Hence, Nowell-Smith advices us better to abandon the assumptions that all words mean the same thing and all adjectives stand for properties. It is better on our part, as he states, to say that "what does so and so mean by the word"? To quote Nowell-Smith himself, For the question "what does the word mean ? I shall, therefore, substitute the two questions : 'for what job is the word '_____' used ? and under what conditions is it proper to use this word for that job?"[8]

Nowell-Smith divides words into different categories according to their jobs and contexts. He makes three categories of words namely, *D*-words, *A*-words and *G*-words. The function of *D*-words or descriptive words according to him is simply to descibe something. They just indicate that an object has certain qualities or properties. For example, the words 'Chair', 'Rose', 'Sun', 'Tall', etc. are *D*-words. In contrast to these, *A*-words are the words which Nowell-Smith calls 'Aptness words', because they are 'words that indicate that an object has certain properties which are apt to arouse a certain emotion or range of emotions.[9] It is quite clear that *A*-words according to Nowell-Smith have an emotive element in them. *G*-words are according to him the gerundive words.

G-words, as he explains, have an element of 'ought' or imperativeness. They command or encourage a person to do something about an object. Words like 'Praiseworthy', 'Laudable' are G-words. The function of G-words is different from that of D-words and A-words. Unlike them they are employed to evaluate something. But like A-words, G-words too do not stand for any quality of an object.

Nowell-Smith has repeatedly stressed the point that moral words which can also be called as 'Value words', such as 'good', 'bad', 'right', 'wrong', etc. Play different roles in different contexts, the main of which are decision, choice, criticism advice, praise, and so on and so forth. The principle that value words mean differently in different contexts Nowell-Smith calls the 'Janus-Principle". He writes, Since I shall make frequent use of the principle that a given word. . . . presumed to be doing two or more jobs at once, I shall give it the special name 'Janus-Principle,".[10]

Ethical words thus have multi-functional jobs to perform according to Nowell-Smith. Some other ethical philosophers also before Nowell-Smith seem to have recognised this fact about ethical terms when they say that 'good' is used not merely to explain or describe something, but also to express some kind of attitude towards an object or to prescribe something to someone. Nowell-Smith classifies the preceding views regarding the meaning of ethical terms as objective and subjective and points out that they represent extreme stand points. The subjectivists have ignored the contextual background and the objectivists have treated this background as the name. Hence, both of them should be synthesised. The connections between the different jobs of value-words are partly logical and partly empirical. If, for example, somebody says "I choose *'A'* and, therefore, I advise you to choose *"A"*, there is, of course, a connection here between choosing and advising but it is not a rigidly logical or analytical connection. It may as well happen that I choose *'A'*, but advise someone else to choose *'B'* instead of *'A'*. Though it seems somewhat logically odd to do so, but it may happen. So the relation between choosing and advising in the above example is a special type of relation which may be called 'quasi-logical'."

Nowell-Smith talks of an implication other than the ordinary implication of a deductive nature. He talks of 'contextual implication' instead of logical implication, while discussing the relation between the premise or premises and the conclusion of an ethical argument. In contrast to logical implication, contextual implication depends purely on context in which the argument occurs. We have seen that Nowell-Smith believes the meaning of a word (specially A-word) depends on context. In the same way the conclusion of an ethical argument is also contextually implied by the premises. Explaining the notion of contextual implication Nowell-Smith writes, "I shall say that a statement *P* contextually implies a statement *Q*, if any one who knew the normal conventions of the language would be entitled to infer *Q* from *P* in the context in which they occur".[11]

Ethics is a practical science. It cannot be evaluated under the formula of 2+2=4. At the same time it cannot be ignored. It is concerned with day-to-day human actions, which again depend on situations. Hence, moral terms have several meanings and moral propositions perform different action in different context.

Thus, Nowell Smith's multifunctionalism or his doctrine of Janus principle is an 'Advance form of Prescriptivism'[12] and a logically consistent theory in ethics.

REFERENCES

1. R. M. Hare, *Philosophy*, Vol. 31, 1956, p. 89.
2. N. Smith, *Ethics*, Penguin Books Ltd., 1954, p. 61.
3. *Ibid.*, p. 98.
4. R. B. Brandit, *Ethical Theory: The Problem of Normative and Critical Ethics,* p. 232.
5. N. Smith, *op. cit.*, p. 63.
6. *Ibid.*, p. 68.
7. *Ibid.*, p. 67.
8. *Ibid.*, p. 69.
9. *Ibid.*, p. 72.
10. *Ibid.*, p. 100.
11. *Ibid.*, p. 80.
12. H. J. McCloskey, *Meta-Ethics and Normative Ethics*, Martinus Nighoff, The Hague, 1969, p. 85.

Chapter – 12

Moral Responsibility and Free Action

Anamika

Ludwig Wittgenstein's philosophy though holistic has two parts, one that can be said and the other that cannot be put into words or the unsaid. According to Wittgenstein, our language has its own limitations. It can say something clearly but there are certain other things which cannot be said clearly. In the *Tractatus Logico-Philosophicus*, Wittgenstein feels that we should remain silent about what cannot be said clearly.[1] But in his later works, he has tried to say the unsayable by thrusting against the limits of language. But he still feels that the more we say, the more still remains to be said. Ethics, aesthetics, culture and religion form part of the unsayable, toward which the sayable always points . So, both are important and cannot be read in isolation.

My point is that Wittgenstein's concern for logic and language leads to his concern for value. What cannot be said, can be shown, e.g., an action in which the will itself becomes part of the action, cannot be described except through action itself. Wittgenstein's views on moral responsibility and free action are also part of the unsayable.

The concept of moral responsibility and Free-action is directly related to the problem of free-will. It is very interesting to note that we find reference to the freedom of will in the *Tractatus* itself. Wittgenstein's views regarding freedom of will are very clear. In the proposition 5.1362, he says :

> The freedom of the will consists in the impossibility of knowing actions that still lie in the future. We could know them only if causality were an inner necessity like that of logical inference. The connexion between knowledge and what is known is that of logical necessity.

Before this proposition, Wittgenstein has already rejected the possibility of inference between the events of the present and those of the future. This makes Wittgenstein declare that the belief in the causal-nexus is a superstition.[2] From David Hume onwards philosophers have been doubtful whether any necessary connection between the past and the future could be established.

Similarly, for Wittgenstein, there is no causal-connection between will and action. Wittgenstein regards willing and acting one and the same thing. So, there are no causes of action. Intention, desire, etc., are prior to action but they are different from will. What is prior to will is only a wish. It may be accomplished or may not be. Willing is acting. So, when we come to the question of ascribing responsibility for our actions, we see that we cannot ascribe responsibility for intentions. We cannot move the world and our own body by mere intentions and wishings. Wittgenstein's view is that we cannot and should not ascribe. We should only describe the state of affairs. For H.L.A. Hart[3] the primary function of action sentences is to ascribe responsibility, even in non-legal claims and judgements. But Wittgenstein would say that responsibility can be fixed only in a game and not outside it. And there is no outside, i.e., no ideal unshakable and eternal. In other words, every action sentence has a different language-game. Ascribing moral responsibility for an action can be possible only from within a game. For example, when a soldier kills an enemy on a war front it is not called murder and hence his action is not defeasible.

Again, sometimes, there can be other bodily movements other than the willed action. Are we to be held responsible for them also? Wittgenstein would ask. Sometimes it may happen that our willed action leads to another state of affairs. For example, we run in panic and kill many people in a stampede. That is to say that we are responsible for certain actions, though we have not directly caused them. Of course such actions are "defeasible", to use Hart's legal term, i.e., actions wherein claims of having performed an action, like claims of having entered into a contract can be overridden or weakened, as for example, going back on promises made or not making the payment on an appointed date and time. Hart's discussion of defeasible action is obviously legal, particularly in the area of contract law. He believes that since defeasible concepts violate the contractual basis, they are ascriptive. He believes that no set of purely descriptive statements perform an action. What is being ascribed to an agent in claiming that he has performed an action for bringing about a certain state of affairs is responsible. Hart's ascriptive view is not causal but moral and social. Action, accordingly, is a bit of behaviour interpreted within the context of moral and social rules and practices.

So, both Hart and Wittgenstein agree on this point that while ascribing responsibility, we have to observe the performance of the action and not to search for any hidden intentions. But otherwise, Hart's view of 'defeasibility' is not very sound. Joel Feinberg[4] says that even in cases where we use such strong words as "murder", we are not justified in calling someone a murderer unless it is proved.

Hart borrowed the term "defeasibility" from the law of property where according to Feinberg, it is used to refer to a estate or legal interest in land which is subject to termination or "defeat" in a number of contingencies but remains intact if no such contingency matures. Hart extends its meaning to cover all legal claims that are regarded as provisionally established at a certain stage of litigation process, but still vulnerable to defeat, annulment or revocation at some later stage of proceedings. Defeasibility, then, is closely associated with the legal notion of "a *prima facie* case", wherein a litigating party is said to have *prima facie* case when the evidence in his favour is sufficiently strong for his opponent to be called upon to answer it. Feinberg thus argues that "the notion of defeasibility then is inextricably tied up with an adversary system of litigation and its complex and diverse rules governing the sufficiency and insufficiency of legal claims, perscriptive conclusive evidence, the role of contending parties and the burden conclusive evidence, the role of contending parties and the burden of proof."[5] We do not have this kind of fool-proof legal system for the social norms. If someone's indifference injured my feelings, I have no court of law to seek remedy. Nevertheless, I feel injured and my friend's behaviour is by all means, defeasible.

But social norms are not binding. Even legal rules are subject to newer interpretations. Moreover, there are certain character-faults which do seem to be defeasible, while there are a number of other character-faults that are non-defeasible, e.g., humourlessness. Again, suppose, we intend to help someone, but when we judge him in public performance, we keep quiet and instead help someone whose performance is comparatively good. Thus, Wittgenstein would simply say that our intentions are hidden and so, it is impossible to judge action on the basis of intentions. So, there is no super strong connection existing between the act of intending and the thing intended.[6] Thus, every action is a new action. Every action is a game in itself and can be judged accordingly. What is defeasible in one game may not be defeasible in another game.

For Wittgenstein. we are responsible for the movement[7], for willing things to happen, not for our intentions. If intentions were to be the criteria of judging the defeasibility of actions, it is bound to fail because there is an old saying : Good intentions pave the way to hell. In Wittgensteinian framework, there is no emphasis on finding out intentions, motives, reasons and causes, in order to judge the defeasibility of actions. Wittgenstein does not wish to go beyond phenomena to discover motives and reasons in persons and causes in both human and physical world as Nicholas F. Gier has also pointed out in his book *Wittgenstein and Phenomenology*. His phenomenology consists insofar as his view on action is concerned, in observing performance. Life is not logic. Only logic moves in straight line. In life, even if we have certain rules for a certain kind of action, still the result may not be in accordance with what we have assumed. That we are, therefore, says Wittgenstein, entangled in our own rules.[8]

We fix responsibility only in terms of rules and when a contradiction appears as soon as we apply a rule, we are left to wonder at how things turn out against all our expectations.

Similarly the concept of right and wrong are relative. There is no absolute value in the world. We cannot say that an action done like this is *the* right action.

Wittgenstein is against any categorical imperative. He says "what if I do not do it?"[9] Again, we as Wittgenstein would say, live in falsehood, simply because we claim, "It must always be..."[10] This wish to expect things to repeat themselves is, however, prior to every experience. Every action is a new action, but being 'new' does not mean that it is altogether new. The 'new' can be a new point of view, a new situation, etc. The question of responsibility is to be solved every time in a new way. Though Wittgenstein does not deny responsibility for action, but he feels that ascribing responsibility is very difficult.

He is not like Richard Taylor[11] or Novell Smith[12] who deny values and moral responsibility absolutely. But still he feels that in the absence of absolute rules for conduct in the world and the willing subject, not knowing the working of the world, ascribing responsibility is a very difficult task. Philosophy, as he puts it "may in no way interfere with the actual use of language; it can in the end only describe it."[12] This is how Wittgenstein denies ascriptions, except that we are responsible for ourselves, for pronouncing good and evil in the world, devoid of these epithets. Wittgenstein's view of reward and punishment is that reward and punishment should be part of the action itself. The feeling of pleasure while doing an action is reward and feeling of pain in doing an action is punishment.

This is the way of looking at things, not from within a game or the world. He wants us to go out of the world or a game and look at it *sub specie aeterinitatis*, i.e., seeing things in their aspects of eternity. This is what is ethical in the absolute sense of the word. Wittgenstein feels that we owe it to life and the world (they are the same for him) to see it in all aspects, i.e., to see it absolutely whatever it is. It is thus alone that we are absolved of our responsibilities by fulfilling them, leaving no aspect unattended. It is in this sense that Wittgenstein is messianic. He turns to the expansive tradition of Diderot, Spinoza and Burno, in so expanding himself, he also achieves his freedom. God, for Wittgenstein does not reveal himself in the world. On the contrary, God is how things stand.[13] In essence, God is in the world, as the world is in God. Like God, the world is extended, it is infinite. But looking at the world from a limited point of view is to be in bondages; freedom, then, is simply a matter of accepting the universe as it stands in its infinite expanse. As long as our eyes are turned in the direction of finite we are in bondage, Wittgenstein himself achieved this freedom at the end of the *Tractatus*, for he said, that his propositions are steps to climb up beyond them, that he must so to speak, throw away the ladder after he has climbed up it. He must transcend these propositions, and then he can see the world aright, of course, *sub specie aeternitatis*.[14]

For Wittgenstein and also for Sartre there is no noumena hidden behind the phenomena. But even phenomena is transphenomenal, it has infinite aspects. The only way to understand phenomena is to look at them from outside, i.e. *sub specie aeterni*. We can see that post modern thinking, beginning with Derrida has the influence of Wittgenstein and Sartre. Derrida ruptured logo-centrism— the fixed sign-signified relationship and thereby the centre by introducing the element of freeplay. It is thus that the whole post-modern thinking received its impetus from Wittgenstein, Sartre and Derrida. Of the three, Wittgenstein is more radical, particularly in turning mystical. He saw no reason for claiming pre-eminence, for himself or any other person. All aspects of the world are equal, even a stone or a snake or a wasp is significant; whosoever realized this will never want to procure pre-eminent place for his own body or for the human body.

He will regard humans and animals quite naively as objects which are similar and which belong together.[15]

For Wittgenstein, it is not merely Christian charity, but a philosophical faith, that one's freedom lies in being responsible for all. Sartre also reaches the same conclusion that to choose for oneself is also to choose for others. Wittgenstein perhaps had the view of comparative anatomy at the back of his mind when he opened up his heart to the organic and the inorganic world, that things come to the world, reach maturity and die, that in place of a man's hand, we have a horse's hoof. In fact every one of the quarduped is patterned on the same prototype, that nature merely lengthens, shortens, modifies or multiplies the same organ. That is why, he indeed says :

> A stone, the body of a beast, the body of a man, my body, all stand on the same level.[16]

Wittgenstein would concur with Diderot[17] who said that nature like a woman loves to vary her costume; she does not require many different outfits, because she knows how by varying a sleeve or a collar, adding a pleat or letting down a hem, to achieve an infinite variety of effects while using the same pattern. Wittgenstein also refers to the analogous view of changing tastes and fashions for the reason of variety:

> Take the case of fashions. How does the fashion come about? Say we wear lapels broader than the last year. Does this mean that the tailors like them better broader? No, not necessarily. He cuts it like this and this year he makes it broader. Perhaps this year he finds it too narrow and makes it wider. Perhaps no expression (of delight-*R*) is used at all.[18]

Wittgenstein thus finds endless variety in the world and since all are equal, all are equally significant and insignificant :

> As a thing among things, each thing is equally insignificant, as a world each one equally significant.[19]

His quest for free but responsible action has driven him to this pass, that he turns a recluse. We know that he gave up his Cabridge Chair and earlier his property to be distributed among needy writers. He then wandered forth in the remote parts of Austria only to be rescued by friends.

His *Philosophical Investigations* grew out of this speculation that our freedom lies in playing language games without finality. Nevertheless his conclusions about free action are reached long before in the end of his *Notebooks* 1914-16 :

> When a general ethical law of the form "Thou shalt. . ." is set up, the first thought is : suppose I do not do it?[20]

But it is clear that ethics has nothing to do with punishment and reward. So this question about the consequences of an action must be unimportant. At least these consequences cannot be events. For there must be something right about that question after all. There must be a kind of ethical reward and of ethical punishment but these must be involved in the action itself.

And it is also clear that the reward must be something pleasant, the punishment something unpleasant.[21]

REFERENCES

1. *Tractatus Logico-Philosophicus*, Translated by David Pears and B.F. McGuinner (London, Routledge and Kegan Paul, 1961), p. 79.
2. *Ibid.*
3. H.L.A. Hart "The Ascription of Responsibility and Rights", *Proceedings of Aristotelian Society,* Vol. 49, 1948-49, pp. 171-194.
4. "Action and Responsibility", *The Philosophy of Action*, Oxford : Oxford University Press, 1968, p. 96.
5. *Ibid.*
6. *Philosophical Investigations*, ed. G.E.M.Anscombe and R. Rhees, trans.G.E.M. Anscombe, Second Edition, Oxford: Blackwell, 1958, p. 197.
7. *Notebooks*, 1914-16, ed. G.H. von Wright and G.E.M. Anscombe, trans. G.E.M. Anscombe. Oxford : Blackwell, 1961, p. 88.
8. *Philosophical Investigations*, p. 125.
9. *Tractatus*, p.147.
10. *Culture and Value*, ed. G.H.von Wright in collaboration with H. Nyman, trans. Peter Winch. Oxford : Blackwell, 1980, p. 14.

11. "Action and Responsibility", *Action Theory*, ed. by Myks Brand and Brughlas Walton (Boston : D. Reidel Publishing Company, 1975), pp. 293-310.
12. "Action and Responsibility", *Action Theory*, pp. 311-22.
13. *Notebook*, p. 79.
14. *Ibid.*, p.83.
15. *Ibid.*, p.82.
16. *Ibid.*, p.84.
17. Denis Diderot, *Thoughts on the Interpretation of Nature*, 1754.
18. "Lectures on Aesthetics", *Lectures and Conversation on Aesthetics Psychology and Religious Belief*, ed. C. Barrett. Oxford : Blackwell, 1970.
19 *Notebooks*, p.85.
20. *Ibid.*, p.78.
21. *Ibid.*

Chapter – 13

Moral Language and Moral Reasoning

Mixture of Clarity and Obscurity

Asha Mukherjee

The task õf a moral philosopher in "contemporary philosophy" has been not to give a normative theory as they are not "seers", they have no special insight into "moral truth". G.E. Moore believed the ultimate aim of moral philosophy is to articulate, if possible, a rational normative ethical system. And if it is not possible, then to work out why and finally, to limit itself to metaethical analysis. Nowell-Smith is of the opinion that ethics is a study of words and concepts. The question of justification in ethics is the question of stating, elucidating and defending a sound procedure for determining the truth of conflicting moral claims and the soundness of moral arguments. Some of the questions with which contemporary moral philosophy is concerned are .... Is metaethical relativism justified? Is objectivity of moral principles justified? What is meant by calling a moral judgement objective? Are they verifiable in the same way as scientific statements? How to determine the meaning of moral judgements? Moore, Ayer, Stevenson, Nowell-Smith, Hare, to name few of them, do not set forth a moral system, instead they analyze moral concepts and moral theories such as Hedonism, Utilitarianism, Intuitionism, etc. They do not in general make moral statements rather they discuss the meaning and function of such statements. For these people analysis is their sole philosophical task which was not so in traditional moral philosophy. For them, analytic ethics is identical with metaethics or with the epistemology of ethics or with the logic of ethics.

Broadly speaking, all the attempts made in this direction may be categorized in *three categories : Naturalism, Non-Naturalism* and *Non-Cognitivism.* Naturalists believe that ethical terms are definable, without the use of other ethical terms using empirical concepts. Non-naturalists accept that ethical statements are true and false and do not name observable qualities. Ethical statements are not analytical statements but are synthetic *a priori.* Non-cognitivists deny that ethical statements are true or false and say that ethical statements cannot be defined by means of empirical concepts. Ethical statements have some function to perform and the function is different according to different writers like expressing speaker's attitude, expressing the feeling of approval, changing the audience's attitude, issuing prescriptions, declaring one's principles, giving advice and so on.

Naturalistic theories have brought to light various ways in which ethical judgements are grounded on the fulfilment of biological and sociological needs ('more evolved', 'to be pleasant', etc.). While non-naturalist theories have revealed prescriptive aspects of moral concepts that are independent of prudential considerations. The main concern of twentieth century ethical philosophy has been to weave together in a consistent pattern with all the threads. Moore's *Principia Ethics* may be considered as the starting point of this programane, which has the most lasting effect. First three chapters of *Principia Ethics* has deeply affected the contemporary ethics though, his own non-natural cognitivism has not been accepted by most of the philosophers. C.L. Stevenson and R.M. Hare were convinced that Moore's case against naturalism is sound but differed from him by having some other form of non-cognitivism.

Moore on Moral Language

For Moore the primary question is "what is good?" or how to define "good"? He shows that all other moral terms can be defined in terms of "good", but "good" itself is simple, unanalyzable, non-natural characteristic like 'red'. We are either dimly aware of it or we are not, but there is no way of defining it or analyzing it so as to make it intelligible to someone who is not directly aware of it. Moore argues that we will not come to know what good is simply by "discovering what are those other properties belonging to all things which are good". To identify 'good' with any other natural property is to commit the Naturalistic Fallacy. The argument can be formulated in the following manner:

(a) If 'good' were defined as something else then either ethical principles become tautologies or statements about the meaning of the word 'good' or reports on usage.

(b) Ethical principles are neither tautologies nor reports on usage they are synthetic and ethical. They are never analytic or semantical properties.

(c) Therefore, 'good' is indefinable or ought not to be defined as something else.

(d) From (c) it follows that it is a simple notion.

Naturalistic Fallacy may be formulated in the following form :

(i) Naturalistic Fallacy consists in identifying the simple notion by which we mean 'good' with some other notion. (PE p. 58); and

(ii) 'Good' which is non-natural object if confused with something natural object needs a specific name—as it is a specific mistake so common—is Naturalistic Fallacy (PE, p.13).

When Moore says that "good" is not a natural property or object he means by 'natural'—"the one which exists in time" (PE, p. 40).

Naturalistic methods make ethical principles tautologies and thereby make ethics impossible. In fact, although Moore called the mistake the NF his argument is really directed against any attempt to define 'goodness' whether in naturalistic terms or not. For this reason, some writers prefer to call it the *definist's fallacy*. The argument that this is indeed a fallacy is called the *open question argument*. Take anything which is allegedly identical with goodness, says Moore, we substitute for variable *x* in a proposed definition of "good" we can always significantly ask if it is good. "Is happiness good?" If "good" means "happiness" then the question should be meaningless just as to ask whether a father is a male parent.

It can also be looked upon in different way. If the statement "the satisfaction of desire is good" were a definition it would be analytic and it would be contradictory to assert "this satisfies desire but it is not good" ("*x* is good", if analytic) so, it must be synthetic.

It is important to note that although much of the inspiration for the fact-value distinction comes from Moore, he did not deny that goodness and badness were real properties and that true factual statements can be made about them. He did insist, however that goodness was a simple indefinable property. Although, his "open question argument" was influential, it is not very convincing. For the apparent openness of questions about what things are good may be just the product of our ignorance or even corruption. Certain question may seem to be open when really they are not. It is a fact, for example, that water is H_2O, i.e., the property of being water is the property of being H_2O. 'Is H_2O water?' is not an odd question for the one who is ignorant of basic chemistry. Similarly, for all kinds of truths, even if they could not be otherwise, we must be under the illusion that they could be.

Even his notion of 'definition', 'natural' and 'goodness is a simple property like yellowness' are full of problems as argued by many writers it does not limit the importance of the first-three chapters of *Principia Ethica*.

Ayer and Nowell-Smith on Moral Language

The second most important contribution in the field of moral language is by A.J. Ayer in his book : *Language Truth and Logic* where he develops emotive theory of Ethics which is understood broadly as synonymous with non *cognitivist* theory. He rejects both naturalistic and non-naturalistic theories as adequate theories of ethics. 'Ought to do something' is to issue a disguised command. Ethical statements are reports about the speaker's attitude. "*A* is wrong" means "I disapprove of *A*". He believed in the verification principle which required that empirical statements cannot be counted meaningful unless some observation is relevant to its truth or falsity. As a result, metaphysical statements must be reckoned to be without meaning. Value statements in ethics or aesthetics fail to attain the status of genuine statements and are exposed as expressions of emotion with imperative overtones. 'Stealing is wrong' is not analytic and it does not admit of empirical confirmation or disconfirmation, neither true nor false; it is not truth-apt. The function of ethical statements is to express feelings or emotions. For him ethical statements are "pseudo concepts". This might suggest that he was claiming that ethics is nonsense. The fact that they are neither analytical nor empirically verifiable, they are "non-sensical" just as metaphysics. (He has a chapter on "Elimination of Metaphysics", but what about having a chapter on "Elimination of Ethics"?) He was aware of this problem. The idea seems to be that although moral judgements are not literally significant, they are not nonsensical, because they possess emotive significance. Ayer defines "emotive significance" in terms of some observable behaviour the occurrence of which constitutes the expression of the feeling, which seems to violate the generalized version of the verification principle.

In fact, the fact remains that the philosophers who advocated the verfiability of falsifiability (Karl Popper) criterion, were convinced that it is futile to argue over matters on which it is 'in principle impossible' to give empirical evidence and they tried to develop a criterion of meaningfulness that would rule out such questions as whether universals exists independently or are they objectively true, is pleasure a good thing. The verfiability criterion recognizes a sentence as meaningful only if it is in principle possible to cite empirical evidence which would count for or against it. For moral statements are not devoid of meaning but the verifiability criterion does not apply and had 'emotive meaning'. P.H. Nowell-Smith's book Ethics is an example of this attempt. The direct object of Nowell-Smith's study is not practice but knowledge: knowledge of the distinctive uses or roles of moral language or knowledge of the meaning of moral concepts. Nowell-Smith says the task of moral philosophy is to map the relationship of moral words, sentences and arguments; and this is a task, not showing how one statement entails or contradicts another, but of showing that in a certain context it would be logically odd to assert one thing and deny another or to ask a particular question.

Example: *A.* I will pay the butcher.
B. Why?
A. Because, I owe him the money.
B. Why? (Meaning, not 'How did the debt arise?' But 'why is the existence of debt, a reason for paying him?')

In no case the reason given by A which is a statement of fact, entails *A*'s decision to do what he decides to do. Nevertheless *B*'s second question is logically odd as no better reason can be supplied further. He thinks that in *empirical matters we have direct access to truths but not in moral matters*. The truth of a moral opinion would not depend on its coherence with other opinions (as Ross thought, or intuitionists believed). We need to examine the logical behaviour of moral concepts. After examining the logical behaviour, which runs through the entire book he tries to develop a systematic way of resolving conflicts of obligation. He contrasts "is" with "looks" and "feels" and "direct tests" with "Indirect tests". He also brings out an important difference between recognizing a moral property and discovering what colour a thing really has. The colour-blind man is willing to admit his own deficiency; but we cannot admit ourselves to be morally blind in the same sort of way. For resolving the moral conflicts we need to substitute a new logical apparatus that may be more successful. He introduces the concept of "contextual implication" and "logical oddness" in the logic of moral discourse (*Ethics,* chap. 6). "For the concept of logical implication or analytic connection between statements, I propose to substitute the concept of '*contextual implication*' and for the concept of self-contradiction that of '*logical oddness*'. He defines these concepts as "a statement *p* contextually implies a statement *q* if anyone who knew the normal conventions of the language would be entitled to infer *q* from *p* in the context in which they occur". (p. 80) He also formulates the rules of contextual implication. "A question is 'logically odd' if there appears to be no further room for it in its context because it has already been answered".

Stevenson's analysis of moral utterances is also very close to Nowell-Smith's and is naturalistic as he accepts '*A* is right' means "I have an attitude of approval towards *A* and *A* is wrong means 'I disapprove of *A*'. But sentences containing the word 'approve' are so difficult to analysis that it seems perverse to use this notion to explain the meaning of moral judgements which we learn to make. The suggestion that the function of moral judgements was to persuade led to a difficulty in distinguishing their function from that of propaganda (*Ethics and Language*, chap. XI). Some general problems in Nowell-Smith's and Stevenson's account can be raised.

1. Thinking it to be right is not identical with our approval of it.
2. How to introspect other's approval?
3. The attitudes could be mistaken at times.
4. 'I', 'now', 'here's references depend on the person's use.
5. 'I feel approval' and 'I do not feel' are not incompatible but 'Divorce is wrong' and 'Divorce is not wrong', surely have something incompatible.

G.E. Moore in his own way shows that these lead to paradoxical conclusions as some actions would be right and wrong. C.L. Stevenson criticizes Moore's argument and the controversy remains unsettled like most of the philosophical controversies.

Hare on Moral Language

In contrast to A.J. Ayer's emotivist theory, where moral utterances were really expressions of feeling or attitude; they had no factual content and were hence neither true nor false; no rational justification was possible in the case of moral judgements. Hare tries to remove the scandal in various ways. He first noted that logical rules of inference could apply to practical matters as much as to factual one.

For example:

1. Take all the boxes to the station. (Major premise)
2. This is one of the boxes. (Minor premise)
3. Therefore, take this to the station. (Conclusion)

He develops the doctrine of moral judgements which is called "prescriptivism" as for him moral judgements are prescriptive and they guide action. Hare agrees with Moore on naturalistic fallacy. However, according to Hare, there is a secondary descriptive component of moral judgements. When something is called good, it must be so called in virtue of some descriptive property it has. Things cannot be good just for no reasons; a person might be called good because—that is in virtue of the fact that—she is altruistic. If the descriptive part is common to descriptions and prescriptions both then anything which makes a reason good reason in one field must make "good reason in one in another".

Hare has another central element that moral, statements are by their own nature universalizable. Every moral judgement logically commits to a universal prescription. With these two basic criterions for moral judgements he develops the idea of *'imperative logic'* by working out rules and thereby giving the foundation for moral reasoning. From a set of non-normative statements no normative statement can be derived and he tries to suggest that there can be a rational solution of basic conflicts in moral principles. In his second book *Freedom and Reason* he contends to have a morality, we must have freedom; we must have a situation in which each man must solve his own moral problems. Freedom here is worked out as a logical condition for the very moral claims. Hare's theory has been criticized on many account; that it seems to have no account of how we should select the universal prescription we make; that Hare's theory leads to individualism which neglects the fact that any morality will necessarily incorporate the rules of conduct which are necessary for communal living, whatever is universalizable is not moral; that it makes moral reasoning appear to be more arbitrary than it actually is. To say "Nothing that we discover about the nature of moral Judgment entails that it is wrong to put all Jews "in gas-chamber" is a reduction of such a position. In his book *Moral Thinking* he develops the theory defended earlier but adds an explanation and defence to "two level utilitarianism" which allows us to stand by conventional moral principles at the intuitive level which being able if necessary to switch to the critical level if basic principles conflict, or if we encounter hard cases.

In spite of these criticisms and modifications in his position its insights about universalizability and general moral rationality, even if incomplete, seems partially correct. The theory has valuable thing to teach us about how to reason about ethics and shows that such reasoning is not just random, subjective or emotional it is much more complex and one needs to look at the moral phenomena and its complexities more closely. Thus, all these writers have tried to weave together a consistent pattern with naturalistic and non-naturalistic thread and with the help of philosophy, of moral language still the question remains, did we reach a clear understanding of Moral language? My answer is 'no' as well as yes. In some sense we become clearer in our understanding but at the same time by going deeper and deeper and by raising more and more questions we make the whole issue more obscure and more complex. Even the issues which we presumed to be clear at the beginning are more unclear as a result of search for clarity. This is the prize a philosopher of language is bound to pay at the end.

If we look at these issues from a little different perspective, questions about knowledge and belief of moral values are equally important from epistemological point of view and in this sense epistemology also deals with meaning and verification and logic of moral words is also part of epistemology. Moral realism maintains that values are real and they have metaphysical objectivity, epistemic objectivity and logical objectivity. They are universal, truth can be attributed and they are true for all. They accept moral facts. Plato, Richard Price, Thomas Reid, Moore, H.A. Prichard, W.D. Ross are some of them who advocate for this position. On the other hand we have Relativists who claim Values are relative to individual, depend on situation or context and get meaning only within a particular context and no absolute or universal principles are possible in morality. Undoubtedly, there are many shades of relativism as I have argued in another paper. (My paper "Moral Relativisim: The Controversy and Solution", pp. 228-246, in *Truth and Value*, Ed. By Raghunath Ghosh, New BBC, Delhi, 2003).

Moral Language Use of 'Ought'

Let me look at the use of language in moral discourse little more closely. I would limit myself be exploring the behaviour and meaning of 'ought' by having different examples and in different situations the way it is presented in our daily life.

Argument – I

(1) *A* took rupees five hundred from *B* and promised to pay back within a week.

(2) Everyone ought, morally, to pay back his debt and keep the promise.

(3) The week is over.

(4) So, *A* ought, morally, to pay back the debt to *B* and keep the promise.

This is a perfectly valid argument whatever might be our notion of logic. But consider the situation where *A* has no income at present and his son meets an accident. Obviously, he is supposed to use everything he has, borrowed or not, to save his son's life. We then naturally accept the following extension of the argument:

Argument – II

(2*) If *A* pays back *B*'s debt his son will die.

(3*) Every parent ought, morally, to save his son's life.

(4*) Hence, *A* ought, morally, not to pay back his debt.

Note here that (4) and (4*) both are intuitively well justified. But these are contrary to each other and none of these can be rejected.

What is wrong here? It doesn't need a logician or a philosopher to tell us that there is an additional premise in Argument II, namely, (2*) which makes all the difference. But this additional premise admitted in the argument simply overrides premise (2) and in conjunction with (3*) gives us (4*) is justified.

Moral Reasoning, Conflict of Duty and Dilemma

A lay man would not find any contradiction in this. Both of these two arguments are perfectly justified in his opinion. However, there are at least two justifiable reasons (for the philosopher!) to worry about situations like this. It is perhaps the absoluteness, of *A*'s son's death, in (2*) that makes the man on the street so sure. But let us first consider a revised version of Argument - II. Suppose instead of his son, *A*'s log meets an accident. Then the argument looks very different.

Argument – III

(2a*) If *A* pays back *B*'s debt his dog will die.

(3a*) Every owner of a dog ought, morally, try to save his pet's life.

(3b*) So, the owner of the dog, i.e., *A* ought, morally, try to save his pet's life.

(4a*) So, *A* ought not, morally pay back his debt!

Now a lay man won't accept this argument to be valid. He would argue that (3a*) is not good enough reason not to pay back the debt, i.e., to override premise (2). Perhaps he is right, Perhaps, it is not reason enough. So, let us dig a little further. Let us consider the situation where *A*'s son is so attached to his pet that he cannot live without his pet. May be the son was born with some disability and heart problem and the pet was brought to give him company. And death of the dog may cause such a mental agony that it is very likely that the boy will die. So where are we now! Suppose some common friend tells the story to the same man of the street, how will he reason now? The argument may now be the following:

Argument – IV

(2a*) If *A* pays back his debt, his dog will die.

(2b*) If the dog dies, it is very likely that the boy will die.

(3b*) So, the owner of the dog, i.e., *A* ought, morally to try to save his dog.

(4a*) Hence, *A* ought not, morally, pay back his debt.

Now, we can expect that a lay man would agree that, barring the premise (2a*) all other premises are the same and he finds it perfectly acceptable.

It might be argued that it is after all the domain of value and the man of the street has the right to have his own principles and value system. This system may not agree with that of *A*'s. In that case, there will be no standard of decision — no argument will help. The argument leads to moral relativism.

But does it really? We might give our friend a little hope and consider the following argument say argument - V. For, till now, only *A*'s predicament was being considered.

Argument – V

Let us consider *B* being placed in the similar situation i.e. *B*'s son meets an accident. So, *A* ought, morally, pay back his money. But *A*'s dog meets the accident and his son being so attached. . . etc., etc . . . . Our friend would probably say: after all *B*'s son was in the death bed and so is *A*'s. Therefore, *A* ought morally to pay back the money. Hence, from relativism to absolute value!

One can perhaps accept that to a certain extent relativism is acceptable. For our friend might have raised the issue that after all, it was only likely that *A*'s son would have died. But, doctor said that, *B*'s son would surely die. Here even a science or more precisely, the doctor's knowledge is brought in to justify some of the premises. Still the fact remains that even the conclusion depends on the prediction of the science called Medical Science and one very well knows, both are philosophically subject of suspicion. But in the process we have shifted to relativity of the propositions of a science from that of relativity of value.

It should be noted that the difference in the premises are not due to any ethical ground. It is a perfectly declarative sentence and makes a claim about a fact. Still, they lead to the different moral conclusions.

It is for this reason that people started looking for a formal ground, that is, Consistent and valid moral reasoning method, depending on which, one should decide whether a particular argument could be said to be invalid and then probably would look for a different ground for justifying the premises of his argument. This would, of course, be different level of philosophical activity. Nevertheless exercises in moral language and moral reasoning remain important at least to find out what is to be justified and how should we go about it. This is the second reason for being concerned about moral language and moral reasoning. One famous or notorious view is to weigh the consequences and then decide what is to be done. But this could not actually be done, without resorting to an arbitrary 'theory' about the way the world is. Besides, in that case to maintain the fact-value distinction is difficult. We'll have to derive ought from is. That may have quite some justification, as Amartya Sen (Hume's Law and Hare's Rule. *Philosophy*, 41, 1966, pp. 75-78) believes to be the case, it is apparent that some idea of 'consequence' needs to be worked out to embark upon such an activity.

Kant has argued that moral judgements are categorical. And common opinion agrees with Kant in Insisting that a moral man must accept a rule of duty whatever his interests or desires. Thus moral judgements are consequences of categorical imperative, good in itself; "an action as of itself objectively necessary, without regard to any other end." Again, "as necessary in a will which itself conforms to reason as the principle of this will, the imperative is categorical." (*Foundation of the Metaphysics of Morals*, Sec. II trans, by L.W. Beck). Philippa Foot has argued in detail that moral could also be hypothetical imperatives. ('*Morality as a System of Hypothetical Imperatives.*' *Philosophical Review*, 71, 1972). She makes interesting observation regarding the distinction between *ought* judgements and *should* statements and argues that *should* statements can *also be catagorical imperatives and could be "in itself giving us reason to act and moral "Ought" does not have any magic force"* (G.E.M. Anscombe in favour of this). Here, I am not going to discuss whether Philippa Foot is right but the central issue is whether moral statements are in any way different from factual statements and if they are how we determine their truth. In my view moral statements have a basic difference in the sense that they have a kind of openness and a kind of binding force in-built in their nature that needs a special attention.

Moral language in general and reasoning in particular as looked upon normally does not have much place for freedom of an agent. The concept of place, time situation and person are supposed to limit the claim to universality of moral laws but add to agent's freedom at some level or other. There are different levels of freedom in morality, namely metaphysical, meta-exercised and exercised consists in the very being of man. A man is a conscious being, who reflects on what he does and thinks. The very fact that a man has this capacity of thinking otherwise and doing otherwise, making things other than what they are, gives the meaning to his being. To exercise this capacity a man has to give meaning to his own being and distinguish himself from other beings. The second kind of freedom consists in choosing principles. If an agent has moral principle and he believes in moral principle due to some reasons then the agent is free to choose every moral principle depending upon the justification provided by the agent in terms of agent's intending, wanting, believing or interpreting the situation and there is no absolute justification for moral principles. The third kind of freedom operates at the level when the moral principles are agreed upon in the beginning but when applied in the particular situations, different conclusions may be justified which are contrary. In this sense moral judgements and its contrary both are justified. It has been the concern of the moral philosophers and logicians for quite some time to somehow get out of this dilemma — to have the said openness and have moral reasoning in a meaningful sense.

In my opinion, to accommodate moral openness with moral reasoning, we have to have a sense of reasoning and consequently logic which is neither deductive nor inductive but may sensibly be called a modification of non-monotonic logic or default logic. In default logic the context plays an important role, the information regarding the agent's epistemic context given its due importance. I one agent gives more importance to one factor rather than the other, he will have a different moral conclusion. The problems related with conflict of duties and moral dilemmas can also be solved to some extent.

Chapter – 14

Understanding the Moral Agent

D.K. Chakravarty

Man is an intentional agent. He can choose or decide. The characteristic of agency distinguishes him from an object. The inquiry into human action cannot be modelled on enquiry into the behaviour of objects. Events happen, there is no choice in them. The intentional purposive model applies to man when he acts. The conceptual confusion between event and action leads to the view that human action, like the behaviour of objects, is caused. Then why of an event is different from the why of an action. In the case of the former we demand for cause, in the latter case we demand for a reason. Benn and Peters observe, "A human action is typically something done in order to bring about a result or in accordance with a standard. Such action can be said to be done more or less intelligently and more or less correctly only because of the norms defining what are ends and what are efficient and correct means to them . . . . (But events or occurrences) are not appropriately described as correct or incorrect, intelligent or stupid".[1]

We are responsible for our own action. We do not describe an agent by calling him 'responsible'. Responsibility is an ascriptive and not a descriptive concept'. Such concepts have the property of being what Prof. Hart calls 'defeasible' an attribute which may be withdrawn in the light of further evidence. The ascription has reason for making it. The part of the reason for calling a man responsible is the putative freedom of the agent. A person is regarded as morally responsible for an action if he is found to be answerable for it. He is answerable if and only if he is supposed to have done it freely. Thus responsibility presupposes freedom of self. Determinism makes nonsense of moral responsibility. It renders obsolete a whole range of moral expressions central to human thought. To the determinist the self is an individual system of determinate cognitive, conative and emotional dispositions. The action of the self is predictable actualization of a determinate potentiality. But the determinist model of self is inadequate because it does not take into consideration man's desire for novelty, for genuine creation, transcending his determinate nature. The self can never be reduced to a determinate object because it can detach itself, in thought and will, from every objective determination.

Can we then say that the self is free from all constraints? 'Freedom from' is often understood in this sense. But absence of constraint should be understood not from the end of constraint but from the end of feeling or consciousness. A person may seem to be under constraint from outside, but left to himself, does not feel constrained at all. To say that such a person is not free makes no sense. Our stubborn feeling of freedom arises from the consciousness of our otherness from objects. Only a self-conscious being can be an agent. An agent affects the world by actions. The causality of the agent is a unique phenomenon, not found among objects. As C.A. Campbell aptly remarks, "We may lay down, therefore, that an act is a 'free' act in the sense required for moral resposibility only if the agent (a) is the sole cause of the act; and (b) could exert his causality in alternative ways".[2] A voluntary action presupposes the decision of the agent. The evidence for the fact that the self is the cause of our free decision lies in our inner awareness of making decisions. Since it is possible for us to decide otherwise than we have in fact decided, our decision is always logically autonomous. Decision is abrupt. This abruptness expresses freedom. Freedom is a presupposition of decision and through decision, of our acts. at our acts.

Responsibility is related to a role of a man in society is responsible. Role implies duties. A person who does not perform the action proper to his station is irresponsible. Does the role deprive a person of autonomy? To the Existentialist, surrender to a role so that one cannot help doing what one does, is a bad faith. Inauthentic identification with a role reduces a man to a standardized entity. But, it is possible to stand back and see oneself playing the role and freedom consists in the capacity to stand back and not to allow actions to be totally determined by the role. Genuine role-responsibility cannot be understood apart from self-responsibility. A man must freely accept the role which must not be imposed on him. If role-responsibility does not Involve self-responsibility, freedom and responsibility will oppose each other. Advocates of self-responsibility speak of 'freedom from'. But 'freedom from' cannot be understood apart from 'freedom to' which role-responsibility presupposes. Any role or way of life laid down for an individual may be abandoned by him. He can transcend any role by all ultimate choice. In this lies his essential freedom. Given a situation-value or fact, to decide this way rather than that makes sense. It is our freedom of decision, and not some determinate cognition, which explains our ideals.

Decision has its limit; the primary limit is due to the human body. As an agent I regard my role as a framework within which I decide what to do. But, what is to be noted is that when I say I am responsible for the action, my action is to be understood as due not to some factual character of the situation but rather to an ideal which 1 bring to bear upon this type of situation. In Hartmann's view, my moral freedom consists in having a determinant of my own and the capacity to add this unique determinant as a Plus not only over and above the determination of causal nexus of events but also over and above the determination of Ought in deciding for or against an Ought[3]. From this point of view, the self is an individual, indeterminate and unconditional power of Self-determination. Its action is the actualization of that power. We live in a seething cauldron of possibilities. Choice is not possible in absence of alternative possibilities of action. But choice is not lust giving assent to a course of action determined by various empirical circumstances. As Kalidas Bhattacharyya puts it, "Given a particular tendency determined by empirical circumstances there is tire choice to submit to it or not". He says further, "it is this choice not to submit which constitutes real freedom and it does not clash with complete determination at the empirical level". "Herein" as Bhattacharyya elaborates, "precisely we have the idea of freedom as transcendeence. Free man transcends nature. He is overnatural even though otherwise he is a part of' Nature, too".[4]

Man's unconditioned freedom carries with itself a responsibility. This responsibility is nothing but the urge to turn the possibility of freedom into an actuality. We are free either to exercise our capacities or not to do so. Therein lies our responsibility. The awareness of this crushing responsibility is what existentialists call 'anguish'. We seek to evade responsibility by pretending that we are not free, that we have no choice, that we are powerless victims of fate, of heredity, of society, etc. In this flight from freedom lies the germ of all kinds of authoritarianism.[5]

In a society where irrationality prevails and events happen by chance without being governed by laws, no man can he responsible. In a society devoid of all constraints moral problems do not arise. Responsibility demands alternatives within the rational bounds of a situation. The moral agent does not live in an absolutely private world. He is not a separatist ego. He is essentially with others. The basic notion of morality is neither that of 'I and You' but that of 'We' which is the same as 'I with others'. Hence in making a choice I act as the representative of mankind. Through the depersonalization of responsible choice I show my authentic existence.

REFERENCES

1. S.I. Benn and R. Peters, *Principles of Political Thought,* Free Press of Glencoe, N.Y. 1965, p. 234.
2. C.A. Campbell, 'Is Free Will a Pseudo-Problem'? *Mind*, 1951.
3. Nicolai Hartmann, *Ethics*, Allen and Unwin, London, 1951, Vol. III, p. 208.
4. Kalidas Bhattacharyya, 'Freedom', *Visva-Bharati Journal of Philosophy*, Vol. II, No. 2, 1971.
5. See Erich Fromm, *Escape from Freedom*, Holt, Rinehart and Winston, N.Y., 1965.

Index